Perspectives
on
Race, Ethnicity, and Power
in
Maritime America

Papers from the Conference Held at Mystic Seaport

September 2000

Edited by Glenn S. Gordinier

MYSTIC SEAPORT · THE MUSEUM OF AMERICA AND THE SEA

Mystic Seaport
75 Greenmanville Ave., P.O. Box 6000
Mystic, CT 06355-0990

www.mysticseaport.org

First edition

Race, Ethnicity, and Power in Maritime America (2nd : 2000 : Mystic, Conn.)

Perspectives on race, ethnicity, and power in maritime America: papers from the conference held at Mystic Seaport, September 2000/edited by Glenn S. Gordinier.–1st ed.–Mystic, CT : Mystic Seaport, ©2005.

p.: ill.: cm.

Includes bibliographical references and index.

1. Minorities–United States–Congresses. 2. Ethnicity–United States–Congresses. 3. United States–Ethnic relations–Congresses. 4. United States–Race relations–Congresses. 5. African Americans–History–Congresses. 6. Garvey, Marcus, 1887-1940. 7. Amistad (Schooner). I. Gordinier, Glenn S.

E184.A1 R3.3 2005

ISBN 0-939510-99-5

Contents

Introduction

Over the last two decades, social history has had a growing impact on the study of American maritime history. What were once the stories of merchants, shipmasters, and the vessels they operated have become the stories of every type of mariner, male and female, rich and poor, the powerful and the lowly. The work of select scholars such as Martha Putney and Herbert Aptheker laid the foundation for a growing body of work that examines questions dealing with social history in the maritime environment. More recently, books by Daniel Vickers, Marcus Rediker, Lisa Norling, and others have further advanced the study of social history issues in the maritime context. Most importantly, regarding race, W. Jeffrey Bolster's *Black Jacks: African American Seamen in the Age of Sail* brought new and intriguing questions to bear on the question of race in the Western Atlantic. Other scholarship has followed, including Julie Winch's biography of the prominent black sailmaker and entrepreneur, James Forten, and Michael Sokolow's biography of Charles Benson, an African American mariner long lost in the folds of history.

Building on the momentum of such scholarship, approximately 250 participants came together at Mystic Seaport in September 2000 for the second national conference titled "Race, Ethnicity, and Power in Maritime America." Previously, a committee had been formed to chart a course for the gathering, and a small cadre of scholars and authorities from across the country were invited to assist in the planning. With the advice of Dr. Dwayne Williams of Susquehanna University, Capt. Bill Pinkney of the Freedom Schooner *Amistad*, Dr. James Miller of the University of South Carolina, Dr. Earl Mulderink of Southern Utah University, Dr.

James Horton of George Washington University, and J. Revell Carr, president of Mystic Seaport, this writer identified a series of goals for the conference. It was agreed from the outset that, although professional scholars would predominate on the rostrum, educators, practitioners of public history, and graduate students would also be invited to answer the call for papers. It was agreed, too, that teachers and the general public would actively be encouraged to attend the conference. Additionally, the chairs of the sessions were specifically instructed to encourage a dialogue between panel members and the audience. The committee also felt strongly that the event should not shy away from the challenges and differing perspectives that can arise when speaking openly about issues of race, ethnicity, and power in this nation's past. They are, after all, almost always closely linked to issues of race, ethnicity, and power in the nation's present.

The call for papers was distributed to those who were engaged in the study of American history and literature, the social sciences, urban, Native American, African American, and Latin American studies, as well as to teachers at all levels. The announcement stated that Mystic Seaport and the planning committee were seeking to engage people "in a broad, cross-disciplinary conversation about issues of race and ethnicity in the American maritime past."

As outlined below, the ten essays in this volume represent the breadth of the papers selected for inclusion in the conference. They are almost universally the creations of professional historians, but they cover a wide variety of America's maritime experiences. For instance, the pieces reflect various locations, including New England, the Middle-Atlantic coast, the Outer Banks of North Carolina, the Gulf Coast, the Mississippi River, and the Caribbean, as well as the factories of Guangzhou (Canton), China. They also range through time from the colonial era to the second half of the twentieth century. Varied approaches to telling the story of America's maritime past are included here as well, including literary criticism, historical interpretation, the social sciences, and an African American community heritage tour. It is hoped that these pages will illuminate regions of our combined past that have previously been obscured, and that they might further advance the conversation that was so enthusiastically initiated in September of 2000.

1.

The challenge of the young United States establishing itself as a worthy member of the international community preoccupied members of the founding generation and its progeny. In "American Expatriates in Canton: National Identity and the Maritime Experience Abroad, 1784-1850," Dane Morrison uses maritime affairs—specifically American traders in China—as a lens through which to examine expressions of national character. As representatives of a nation recently made out of whole cloth, American seafarers in the late eighteenth and early nineteenth century were very sensitive to signs from others regarding their homeland's legitimacy, and in the factories of Canton, living and working cheek-by-jowl with merchants from Europe's great powers, this was especially the case. These "new men," as Crevecoeur called them, accepted the social theories of the day, which held that nations could range from the primitive to the genteel, and on to the decadent. The character these American expatriates appropriated for their own was the "True Yankee," a man who might be new to the scene but who could appreciate and deserve claims to gentility. These True Yankees draped themselves in the racist and nationalist jargon of the period, particularly when seeing themselves surrounded by the corruption that pervaded the Celestial Empire. Morrison helps us see how these world travelers reinforced the virtue of their new American Republic by the language they applied to the "other."

2.

In recent decades it has become common for historians to draw on the methodologies of other social sciences. Economics, anthropology, sociology, and others have all been tapped to allow historians to cast their nets wider and to analyze the historical record in a variety of intriguing ways. In her chapter, "'Poor fellow, I sencerly wish him well': Peter Woodward's Life Course in Nineteenth-Century Philadelphia," Janet Harrison Shannon turns to the work of an influential psychologist to help her interpret the life of an obscure African American who sought to make his way in a maritime community. Shannon applies Dr. Glenn A. Elder's concept of "life course" to the personal story of Peter Woodward, a young African American who was brought to the City of Brotherly Love. "Life course" as developed by Elder seeks to understand human development across the lifespan, and how individual lives can be socially patterned over time, including how lives are influenced by changing environments.

Peter Woodward arrived in Philadelphia in 1785 at the age of eleven. He was taken into the home of Elizabeth and Henry Drinker, a prosperous and influential Quaker couple. It is largely through the pages of Mrs. Drinker's extensive diary that we catch glimpses of Woodward's life course, and in the process are able to see how elements such as time, location, and race play central roles in influencing the lives and opportunities of individuals. Through her application of secondary sources, city and federal records, and most especially the Drinker diary, Shannon adds another small section to the tapestry of America's maritime past.

3.

Professor Julie Winch's contribution to the study of race, ethnicity, and power in maritime America, "'No Common Lot': An African-American Sailor's Half-Century at Sea in the Age of Sail," keeps us in the seaport of Philadelphia, Pennsylvania. In that community, Peter Woodward had little influence, but during much of the nineteenth century the name Forten identified influential African Americans in both business and political realms. James Forten (1766-1842) was one of the nation's most successful black entrepreneurs. The owner of numerous properties, he was best known for his large and successful sail loft. His youngest son, William Deas Forten, later became an important political figure in postbellum Philadelphia. These two men, however, were not typical of the many thousands of African Americans who sought work in the urban centers of the eastern seaboard. As the work of Putnam, Bolster, and others has shown us, of those thousands, a large number became common seamen. This was the case with James Forten Dunbar, nephew and namesake of the elder Forten. Winch recently authored an extensive biography of James Forten, and in doing so tapped materials that led her to uncover Dunbar, a seafarer of color who highlights both the opportunities and the limitations that confronted many of his peer group. And, where Shannon's Peter Woodward dallied with seafaring, Winch's Dunbar used it as his singular life course even into old age, serving on a variety of sailing ships as both a merchant mariner and a naval seaman.

4.

Jazz has often been touted as America's gift to the musical world. Exported from New Orleans, it matured in the cities of the North and influenced the world's sensibilities. But the transport of that musical style was not only via railroad, automobile, or bus. It also traveled on the rivers of America's central basin. In "Jazz on the Waterways: Movement, Migration, and Music," drawn from his forthcoming book, William Kenney describes the vibrant and dynamic environment of the Mississippi River excursion boats and their central role in bringing jazz to the nation's heartland. Just as the waters of the Mississippi's tributaries mixed and swirled, so too did the social and cultural dynamics of America as Jim Crow and the Jazz Age shared both space and time. The riverine environment of the Streckfus Steamship Line and its massive excursion craft allowed skilled black musicians like Louis Armstrong and Fate Marable to spread the gospel of jazz upstream and to a whole new audience. Stomping away on the expansive dance floors of the Streckfus steamers, white audiences by the thousands responded to the syncopations and driving rhythms of New Orleans jazz. Kenney explores the promise and the limitations that new and untried contact with the "other" brought when successful and self-possessed black musicians and their white audiences met face-to-face while cruising on the Mississippi. He considers as well the tensions between the possibilities that travel on the great river afforded, the difficulties of the Great Migration, and the changing character of America that was heralded by jazz.

5.

There are many ways in which maritime history reflects larger historical currents, such as nation-building. In their paper, "Sailing, Shipping, and Symbolism: Marcus Garvey and the Black Star Steamship Line, 1916-1922," Marifrances Trivelli and Dwayne E. Williams "highlight the intersection of race, maritime life, and African American history." They accomplish this by examining how Marcus Garvey's Universal Negro Improvement Association operated its racially based Black Star Steamship Line. The forward-thinking Garvey understood the value of gravitas for his African nation-in-waiting. He understood, too, that one entity that brings legitimacy to a nation is a merchant marine. As a result, he established the Black Star Line. In serving as tangible evidence of the potential of Pan Africanism, the shipping line was enthusiastically received by African Americans. Life was given to the dream as tens of thousands of supporters donated over $750,000 to the capitalization effort. But, unfortunately, the experiment was doomed to failure.

Trivelli and Williams argue that the rise and fall of the Black Star Line is best understood within the broader social, political, economic, and cultural contexts that were mediating the lives of black people in the years following the First World War, and in their piece they examine how the goal of nation-building conflicted with commerce and ship operations. They close their chapter by considering the legacy of the Black Star Line and the lasting impact it had on some of those who were involved in its operation.

6.

For many in twentieth-century America, impressions of the "other" were largely fashioned by the mass media. Radio, cinema, and television all helped the public create popular images of everything from Rick's Casablanca to the cowboy "West" of Dale Evans and Roy Rogers. One of the most influential sources for imagery of the exotic, however, was *National Geographic Magazine.* From 1948 to 1970, one of that trusted serial's oft-published photographers and essayists was Carleton Mitchell, the man who popularized Caribbean cruising. In her essay, "Carleton Mitchell and the Rhetoric of Seagoing Dreams," Rosalee Stilwell examines Mitchell's work and how his particular sensibilities, and those of *National Geographic*, influenced mid-century America's understanding of the Caribbean and its people. Based on her contacts with Mitchell, and on the collections at Mystic Seaport, Stilwell compares Mitchell's two seminal works about sailing through the West Indies, along with the images they proffer to the reading public. Through these two compilations of words and images, Stilwell expands on the work of Catharine Lutz and Jane Collins as she analyzes the ways in which the magazine article and the book differ, yet present their two readerships with appealing and influential versions of a dream-like truth. In doing so, Stilwell examines how epideictic rhetoric in these two pieces resulted in two contrasting but informative visions of race and ethnicity in the twentieth-century Atlantic World.

7.

The littoral border, whether on the Atlantic coast, along the banks of the Mississippi, or in the harbors of the Caribbean, is where land and water rub up against each other. In that environment of flux, peoples have done the same. This has most certainly been the case in the great entrepôts of the Americas. The gifts of the sea have meant that lesser harbors of refuge and portals to opportunity have seen the high-energy dynamics of varied peoples living and working in close proximity. Deanne Stephens Nuwer examines these dynamics in her chapter, "The Mississippi Gulf Coast: Casting a Wide Cultural Net." Nuwer finds Biloxi, Mississippi, to have been profoundly shaped by neighboring Gulf waters, and the history and ethnic makeup of that community is directly related to the influence of its littoral character. The early heritage of the Mississippi coast has included influences by Native American, French, Spanish, Caribbean, African, British, Irish, and Scottish residents, all of whom have contributed to Biloxi's multicultural personality. Within the last century, however other ethnic groups have enmeshed themselves in Biloxi's cultural net. Oystering and then shrimping attracted Slavonians from the Dalmatian coast, who were joined by

Poles, Acadians from neighboring Louisiana, and, more recently, Vietnamese. These groups found their niche in the local maritime economy, created social clubs, founded churches, and shared in the rich environment and multiethnic heritage that has always characterized this section of the littoral.

8.

David Cecelski's "The Last Daughter of Davis Ridge: Slavery and Freedom in the Maritime South" introduces the reader to a corner of the Atlantic World that was at one moment both unique and representative. His paper subsequently became the afterword of a larger work, *The Waterman's Song: Slavery and Freedom in Maritime North Carolina.* The abandoned community of Davis Ridge was located on a hammock in the vast salt marsh system northeast of Beaufort, behind North Carolina's Outer Banks. Founded by runaway slaves during the Civil War (when Union forces captured Beaufort in 1862), Davis Ridge prospered until the 1930s, its residents garnering a living by menhaden fishing, oystering, boatbuilding, "saltwater farming," and home production.

As in many other isolated communities, the African Americans of Davis Ridge interacted with their neighbors through, trade, barter, and the exchange of skilled production. The coastal environment in which they lived, and the independent nature of working the water, also allowed this black community to maintain its social and economic identity in spite of the threats and restrictions that were so prevalent in Jim Crow North Carolina. Cecelski, himself a native of the region, relates the unique character of Davis Ridge, a maritime community in which blacks and whites lived and worked in unusual collegiality. Their churches, fish camps, and even homes witnessed an unprecedented exchange across the color line, and the influence of the sea on this community of color on the littoral was fundamental to its development and its character.

9.

Another American Atlantic community that was separated from the influence of the larger world was that of Martha's Vineyard. Located a few miles off Cape Cod, Massachusetts, the Vineyard has relied on its maritime nature for much of its livelihood and identity. However, the modern history of the island and its people is the history of the dominant culture. Since the early seventeenth century, that culture has been white, Protestant, and patriarchal. As a result, the history of Native and African Americans on the island has largely been lost over the years. In an effort to rectify that deficiency—and informed by the work of Ronald Takaki, Howard Zinn, and others—Elaine Cawley Weintraub began to address this loss of history on Martha's Vineyard in 1989. Her essay, "'Where Were all the Black People Then?': The History of the African American Heritage Trail of Martha's Vineyard, and Its Role in the Education of the Community of the Island," reports on the process of creating such a public history entity and relates the stories of those commemorated by the trail. Weintraub acknowledges her reliance on the concept of Action Research, as described by Kemmis and McTaggart in their 1989 volume, *Action Research Planner.* Weintraub's work uncovered enslavement on the island, the lives of unsung mariners of color, and people who played a vital role in the development of the island's community of color.

10.

Just as the memory of individuals or groups can become clouded or laden with the presumptions or assumptions of others, so can the recollection of events. The resultant misunderstandings can then be exacerbated when fictionalized versions of the happening, with their varied and often unspoken meanings, are offered to the public. In "The Perilous Voyage of the *Amistad* in History and Memory," Robert S. Wolff considers the recently popularized *Amistad* incident of 1839-41 and seeks to cast light into the shadows that envelop such an event when popular culture, mass markets, and an author's or screenwriter's creativity collide with the historical record. By examining Steven Spielberg's film *Amistad,* contemporary published versions of the incident, and the documented record, Wolff challenges us to ponder how historical meaning can be distorted through the mass media. As he unpacks the several accounts of the *Amistad* affair and their conflicting interpretations, he reminds the reader that in the name of accuracy, both scholar and screenwriter alike must understand and acknowledge the influence of the environment in which any such event takes place. The struggle of the African captives within the American judicial system, Wolff explains, must be examined within the context of the Atlantic World of the early nineteenth century.

The Second National Conference on Race, Ethnicity, and Power in Maritime America was championed by Steven T. Florio and made possible in part by a grant from Condé Nast Publications, Inc., New York, as is this volume. We are grateful for the generous support.

  Members of the administration of Mystic Seaport, who envisioned and supported every effort to advance these studies, deserve to be commended as well. So too do those who enthusiastically committed themselves and their creativity to this project. Particular thanks go to Andrew W. German, director of publications at Mystic Seaport, who helped shepherd this work to fruition. Connie Stein, publications administrative assistant, was also of the greatest help. Designer Ben Kann and Dr. Mary K Bercaw Edwards, who served as final copyeditor, are also deserving of our gratitude.

Glenn S. Gordinier
Editor

Contributors

David Cecelski, Ph.D., is the Lehman Brady Joint Chair Professor in Documentary and American Studies at Duke University and the University of North Carolina, Chapel Hill. His chapter in this volume appears in his recent work, *The Waterman's Song: Slavery and Freedom in Maritime North Carolina*, University of North Carolina Press, 2001.

William Kenney, Ph.D., is a professor of history at Kent State University. He has published numerous scholarly articles regarding the history of American music. His contribution in this volume is drawn from his forthcoming book, *Jazz on the River: Music, Race and the Parade of Power on the Mississippi and Ohio, 1907- 1978*, University of Chicago Press, 2005.

Dane A. Morrison, Ph.D., received his degree from Tufts University and is an assistant professor and chair of the History Department at Salem State College. His current interest in the influence of American voyages to the East is reflected in this work. His published works include *A Praying People: Massachusetts Acculturation and the Failure of the Puritan Mission, 1600-1690*, Peter Lang, 1995.

Deanne Stephens Nuwer, Ph.D., is an assistant professor of History Education at the University of Southern Mississippi at Hattiesburg, Mississippi, where she did her advanced studies. Her specialty is pedagogical methods, and she trains students majoring in history who seek licensure in the social studies.

Janet Harrison Shannon, Ph.D., took her degree from Temple University. She is currently an associate professor in Davidson College's Sociology Department. She has lectured and published on issues regarding Black family life, childhood, and church organization in the nineteenth century.

Rosalee Stilwell, Ph.D., is an associate professor in the English Department at Indiana University of Pennsylvania. Her academic interests focus on rhetoric and the study of power and persuasion in human discourse. She has written *The Ethos of Voice in the Journal of James Rainstorpe Morris from the Sable Island Humane Station, 1801-1802*, Edwin Mellen Press, 2000.

Marifrances Trivelli is the director of the Los Angeles Maritime Museum. She earned her M.A. in History from the University of Connecticut. She has written numerous articles regarding maritime topics and is currently researching minority shipbuilders in the Los Angeles area during World War II. Her research for this article, as well as that of **Dwayne E. Williams**, was funded in part by the Paul Cuffe Memorial Fellowship for the Study of Minorities in American Maritime History.

Elaine Cawley Weintraub, Ed.D., is a social studies teacher at Martha's Vineyard Regional High School. A contributor to the local press, Dr. Weintraub has also been a long-time advocate of heritage studies for young adults, and her numerous public history initiatives on the Vineyard are models for including minority voices in public history.

Dwayne E. Williams, Ph.D., took his degree in History and African Studies at the University of Minnesota. Currently an independent scholar, he has served on the faculty of Susquehanna University and Sea Education Association, as well as on the planning committee for the 2000 REPMA Conference. His area of expertise is the Atlantic world and the African diaspora.

Julie Winch, Ph.D., received her degree from Bryn Mawr College and is currently a professor of History at the University of Massachusetts at Boston. Her areas of expertise include Afro-American history and maritime history. She is the author of numerous articles and four books, including *A Gentleman of Color: The Life of James Forten*, Oxford University Press, 2002, which was awarded the American Historical Association's Wesley-Logan Prize.

Robert S. Wolff, Ph.D., received his degree from the University of Minnesota. He is currently associate professor and chair of the history department at Central Connecticut State University. His research focuses upon the social construction of race and national identity in American history. He is completing a book-length study of schooling and society in Baltimore between the Civil War and 1920.

Editor: **Glenn S. Gordinier, Ph.D.**, is the Robert G. Albion Historian at Mystic Seaport, where he teaches for the Williams College/Mystic Seaport Maritime Studies Program and co-directs the Frank C. Munson Institute of American Maritime Studies. He also teaches for the University of Connecticut and coauthored *Fishing Out of Stonington: Voices of the Fishing Families of Stonington, Connecticut*, Mystic Seaport, 2004.

Perspectives
on
Race, Ethnicity, and Power
in
Maritime America

American Expatriates in Canton:

The stars and stripes flies over the American factory at Canton, ca. 1850. (Mystic Seaport 1954.590)

National Identity
and the
Maritime
Experience Abroad
1784-1850

Dane A. Morrison

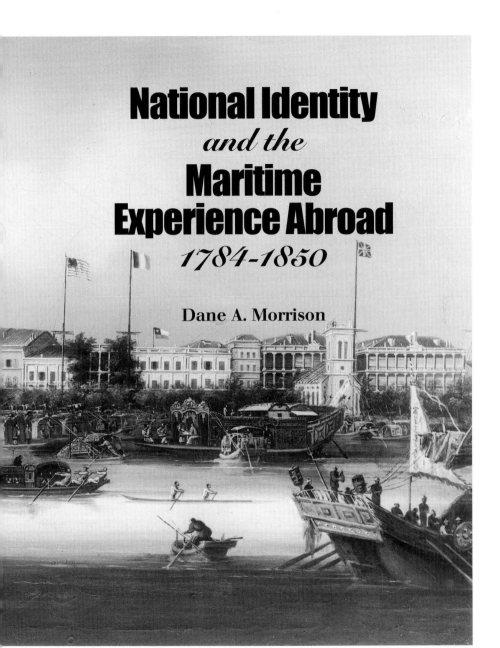

On his second voyage to Canton (Guangzhou), Major Samuel Shaw, serving as first American consul to China, recorded in his journal his observations of the life of a resident merchant in China. Of particular significance for Major Shaw were incidents such as the following, recalling his arrival at Macao, entrance to the Pearl River, in 1786:

A circumstance that occurred at the entertainment given us by the Portuguese ought not to be omitted. The dessert, which was very elegant, was prepared in a room adjoining that in which we dined, and the tables were ornamented with representations, in paper and gilt, of castles, pagodas, and other Chinese edifices, in each of which were confined small birds. The first toast was Liberty! and in an instant, the doors of the paper prisons being set open, the little captives were released, and, flying about us in every direction, seemed to enjoy the blessing which had just been conferred upon them.[1]

Shaw's journal entry is characteristic of the experiences of Americans who resided in Canton during the early years of the Republic and of the meanings they gave to those experiences. It is emblematic, also, of the uses to which the maritime literature of the period represented Americans' encounters with other peoples in the waters of the Pacific. Major Shaw's journal does not tell us if any Chinese guests attended the dinner, nor does the entry offer a glimpse into Chinese reactions to the festivities. The striking element is the way in which Americans experienced Canton, their few acres that constituted the Western factories there, as a cosmopolitan enclave in which the Chinese hovered about them, but in which the salient actors were, like themselves, *fan qui*, "the barbarians from afar." In these descriptions, Canton was the stage, the expatriate community were the actors, and the public sphere of the literate West—Europeans and especially Americans—was the audience. And, although they occasionally played bit parts, the "other"—Indians, Malays, Parsees, and especially the Chinese—were largely props. The Canton experience was part of a larger drama, the search for an American national identity and acceptance within the community of civilized nations. And, it was one that was played out at home

4

and abroad, but especially wherever Americans found themselves among other peoples.

This paper examines the connections between maritime experiences in the Pacific and portrayals of national character depicted in the letters and journals of American expatriates in Canton in the years after the Revolution. It shows that the ways in which American expatriates constructed the peoples of the Pacific were founded in a constellation of ideas, connecting Americans' theories of civilization, their efforts to secure a national identity, and their encounters with the peoples of the Pacific. These plots were especially important for American expatriates, who were anxious to be accepted within what was then called the community of civilized nations. As the paper will show, Americans' "discovery" of markets in the Pacific and Indian Oceans following the American Revolution not only rescued the national economy from a devastating depression, but also launched a buoyant celebration of American character. Commercial exploration of the East seeded a flowering of literary and journalistic constructions which explored the themes of discovery and identity. And, the genre contributed to the development of a nascent national character—the "real Jonathan" or "true Yankee."

THE SEARCH FOR NATIONAL IDENTITY IN THE EARLY REPUBLIC

The construction of a national identity was a conundrum for citizens of the new Republic. Before independence, most colonists thought of themselves as British. Following the Revolution, Americans struggled to create an American identity from the 13 strands of disparate colonial identities. The period between the end of the Revolution and the War of 1812 was a time when the name American as a national label was still unfamiliar to many ears, when people described themselves as Carolinians and New Yorkers, Rhode Islanders and Marylanders, when Thomas Jefferson still referred to his home country as Virginia, and when the "American Farmer," J. Hector St. Jean de Crevecoeur, asked, "What then is the American, this new man?"Americans were sensitive to their *arriviste* status, and in the struggle for recognition that ensued

5

alongside their earliest encounters with the East, searched for signs of legitimacy. So, on the Canton stage, Major Shaw engaged in efforts to publicize the worth of his nation, noting in his journal how the Chinese "styled us the New People, and when, by the map, we conveyed to them an idea of the extent of our country, with its present and increasing population, they were not a little pleased at the prospect of so considerable a market for the productions of their own empire."[2]

Challenges and doubts confronted these "new people" and their republican "experiment" during the early decades of its existence. In the public sphere of literate Americans and Europeans, few political observers, here or abroad, gave its survival much hope. Many close observers of international politics agreed with Frederick II of Prussia, who maintained, "I am much persuaded that this so-called independence of the Americans will not amount to much." Americans grew particularly sensitive to the many public assaults on their character that issued from European quarters. As Federalist politician Fisher Ames recalled in 1800, "Until that contest, a great part of the civilized world had been surprisingly ignorant of the force and character, and almost the existence, of the British colonies. . . . They did not view the colonists so much a people, as a race of fugitives, whom want, solitude, and intermixture with the savages, had made barbarians."[3]

Despite the success of their Revolution and Ames's assumption of newly won respect, Americans were aware that their character as a people remained in question. For instance, in 1784, newspapers such as the *Salem Gazette* carried an offensive report out of New York that "The late English papers represent the people of America as mere brutes and savages, and portray our merchants and traders as destitute of principle, honour, and common honesty." Consequently, Americans were anxious for acceptance into what Europe defined as the community of civilized nations. Situated, in de Toqueville's words, "in the midst of wildernesses, twelve hundred leagues from the main heart of civilization," Americans poured into the public sphere every marker of European acceptance and any slight on their national reputation.[4]

Ultimately, however, what would matter was not so much what was written or said, but rather what this new people could achieve and how they conducted themselves. Many journals observed with distaste the London *Independent Chronicle*'s blithe dismissal of the voyage of the *Empress of China* to Canton in its issue of 29 July 1785, "The Americans have given up all thought of a China trade which can never be carried on to advantage without some settlement in the East Indies."[5] Such slights were countered in the public sphere with vigorous retorts. The *Salem Gazette* of 4 March 1784, offered "A PROPHECY respecting America, not unlikely to be fulfilled . . . . In the year 1800 they will have opened a trade to the East-Indies." In the emergent public sphere of the new Republic, it became important not just to promise illusory achievements, but to show the world what Americans could accomplish.

DISCOVERY AND IDENTITY

Americans found a solution to the perils of statehood, a solution that contributed also to the enigma of national identity; a solution that came through the auspices of an *Empress* and a *Turk*. On Washington's Birthday 1784, the *Empress of China* cleared New York harbor for Canton, "in order to encourage others in the adventurous pursuit of commerce," as merchant Robert Morris informed John Jay.[6] The 360-ton ship carried ginseng, cordage, wine, lead, iron, Spanish dollars, and, as a supercargo or business agent, Major Samuel Shaw of Boston, a former officer in the recent Revolution. When the *Empress* returned to "Yankee land" in May of the next year, she brought a profit of $30,000–a 25 percent return on investment.[7] More than that, the *Empress*'s voyage inaugurated American participation in the China trade. On her return trip to Canton for the 1786-87 season, she berthed among four other American vessels at Canton, including the *Experiment* and the *Hope* of New York, the *Canton* of Philadelphia, and the *Grand Turk*, flagship of a fleet owned by Elias Hasket Derby of Salem.[8] Although the *Grand Turk* would not return to Canton, Derby preferring to ply adjacent realms of the Pacific and Indian Oceans, like the *Empress* she opened a connection between Americans and the exotic worlds "eastward of Good Hope." By 1790, 28 American vessels had voyaged to Canton, and within a decade American trade with the Orient was an established motif in American life.[9]

Commercial exploration of the East seeded a flowering of literary and journalistic constructions that explored the themes of discovery and identity and which filled the public sphere. Through journals, diaries, logs, letters, lectures, and travelogues—much of which is available in Salem's Peabody Essex Museum—American mariners and merchants made places such as Bengkulu, Huangpo, or Jolo Island as familiar to American readers as Salem or Mystic. Through the literature of exotic commerce, the community of maritime adventurers engaged the community of American readers and vicariously shared such adventures as trading blows with pirates in the Straits of Bangka, slinking through Moslem harems in Malaysia, or negotiating *cum shaw* with Canton mandarins.

CONFRONTING THE COMMUNITY OF CIVILIZED NATIONS

Although the public sphere was filling with paeans to "the great American Republic," Americans were aware of their uncertain status as "the new people" in world affairs.[10] As Michael Warner has shown, they felt both a continuing sense of cultural dependence on the Old World and a need for autonomy and authenticity.[11] The citizens of the Early Republic were anxious for acceptance into the community of civilized nations. In constructing a coherent national character, then, they drew upon a set of ideas and experiences that provided commonality among Yankees from across the new land, linkages to what they perceived as the standards of civilized behaviors, and distinction from a constructed "other" who represented characteristics opposed to their own emergent values.

One of the most compelling ideas that informs the maritime literature of the Early Republic is a theory of civilization common to Western thought during the "second great age of discovery." According to this theory, the history of every society was marked by advancement through four stages of economic and social development: from primitive hunting and gathering, to early agricultural, to "modern commercial society . . . characterized by . . . the 'polish' and 'luxury' manufacturing, to decadence." "Of tremendous significance in this formulation," as Drew McCoy has shown, "was the idea that each stage of development was characterized . . . by appropriate and well-defined patterns of human behavior."[12] And, the challenge to those who would knit the society of the Early Republic

8

into a common set of values was to "maintain the country at a relatively youthful stage of development. Hoping to avoid the social evils both of barbarous simplicity and of overrefined, decadent maturity," Americans sought to enscript a statement of national character that established their place and connected this theory of civilization to their "revolutionary ideology."[13] In particular, they hoped to delay for as long as possible the inevitable slide toward a society of decadence and decay, in which, as David Osgood described in a 1795 address in Boston, "arbitrary rulers . . . nourishing their luxury, pride, pomp, and glory with the tears of general misery."[14]

The newspaper reports, memoirs, and essays of resident merchants and sojourning mariners in Canton take on a further level of meaning if we see them in the context of a second salient historic development, one that reached fruition in the early nineteenth century throughout the Western world. This was the emergence of a concept of refined, genteel society. Historians such as Richard Bushman see in the popularization of gentility, "a great movement . . . [which] enabled the [middle] class"–and here we would include the captains, mates, and merchants of early America–to "appropriate many of the honors and privileges of the genteel."[15] Through such media as courtesy books, garden and architectural manuals, art, music, or furnishings, these historians find, "the cultural practices of an aristocratic European society, quite removed from anything known on these shores, flowed into" American society. And, as Bushman notes, "To all appearances, the readers of the books wanted instruction in the arts of genteel living."[16] Coupled to both a popular theory of civilization that maintained that "Men's manners, habits, customs, and morals changed, in other words, as society advanced" and to an urgent quest for national character, the gentility movement had particular resonance in the records of discovery and encounter in the Pacific. Americans in Canton would use their experiences to help construct a national identity that distinguished itself from both the most primitive and the most advanced elements they encountered. The effort to construct a national identity that safely coursed the straits between the primitive and decadent was a dilemma for the mariners and merchants who styled themselves "green Yankees." For American mariners, particularly officers and factors involved in the overseas trade,

9

commerce demanded civility, and the successful merchant needed to demonstrate he was not a sailor or a trader solely, but also a gentleman.

Commercial contacts with other peoples, initiated in 1784 by merchants and mariners of the young Republic, challenged familiar regional frames of reference. They situated American character between the poles of marked European civility and the uncharted customs of exotic peoples. Raising comparisons to the peoples of "Oriental" lands and to Europeans, this literature situated Americans within an "imagined community" of civilized nations, yet distinguished them by their confidence, their zest for adventure, their poise in the face of danger, their devotion to liberty, and their naive openness and unvarnished candor. Thus, in freighting tales such as that of the *Betsey*'s confrontation with Malay pirates to American readers, the maritime literature of the Early Republic celebrated commercial explorers such as Edmund Fanning as the quintessential American character, what became known as the "true Yankee."

The experience of travel to lands unknown gave mariners of the new Republic a clearer sense of the boundaries of their own national character. The publication of these experiences was a significant contribution to a debate over national character that was taking place in the public sphere. Adventuring voyages to distant lands not only opened Americans to uncharted sources of goods, but also introduced them to unfamiliar places, peoples, and experiences. The prospect of Americans in unknown places excited the imaginations of their countrymen. The maritime literature that freighted these tales to the Republic depicted "new worlds" in Americans' consciousness and presented them with images of the fascinating, the curious, the frightening, the revolting.

CONFRONTING THE "OTHER": LIBERTY IN THE PUBLIC SPHERE

In the Indian and Pacific Oceans and throughout the South Seas in the years following the Revolution, American mariners encountered a host of unfamiliar peoples. Through their perceptions of the "other," the literature of discovery contributed to the construction of an "imaginary community" of "true Yankees." The "real

Jonathan" emerged as a set of character traits triangulated between European and non-western peoples, but clearly within the bounds of the civilized peoples of the world. Nowhere in the world was more salient for addressing the problem of identity than Canton. Messages from Canton took on particular prominence and were repeated in newspapers and discussed in the coffeehouses and around dining room tables.

"The Reception Its Citizens Have Met"

As American newspapers boasted of the first vessels to fly the stars and stripes at Canton, up the Hooghly River, through Batavia harbor, or in Manila, logbooks and journals were preoccupied with the question of how they would be received. When the *Empress of China* berthed triumphantly in New York harbor at the end of her first voyage to Canton, one of the first responsibilities Major Shaw fulfilled, on 19 May 1785, was a report to the U.S. Foreign Minister, observing, "it becomes my duty to communicate to you . . . an account of the reception its citizens have met with, and the respect with which its flag has been treated in that distant region."[17]

The writing of the period, both public and private, following Shaw's lead was filled with evaluations of how indigenous peoples, and especially Europeans abroad, treated Americans in exotic ports. For the most part, the Yankees could be pleased. Examples of civil accommodation and polite reception adorned the retelling of virtually every encounter with their European neighbors. As the *Empress of China* had a diplomatic as well as commercial mission, Major Shaw was pleased to report, "The Swedes, the Danes, the Dutch, and the Imperialists [Germans] paid us every proper attention; nor were the English behindhand with them. Besides the gentlemen of the factory, many of their captains visited us, gave invitations, and accepted ours in return."[18]

Even their recent enemies strove to make amends, and Major Shaw wrote, "On board the English it was impossible to avoid speaking of the late war. They allowed it to have been a grave mistake on the part of their nation–were happy it was over–glad to see us in this part of the world–hoped all prejudices would be laid aside, and added that, let England and America be united, they might bid defiance to all the world."[19]

Ascending the Pearl River up to Whampoa anchorage in November 1807, Captain Amasa Delano took note that, "On going up we passed the English frigate *Phaeton*, commanded by Commodore Wood, with several other men of war under his command.We were boarded from the squadron, and treated politely, they offering us any assistance we might be in want of."[20] In August 1798, also in Canton, Captain Edmund Fanning confidently reported that the British East India Company Commodore presented him with an invitation, couched in the most polite and friendly terms,

for myself to accompany these gentlemen, to his ship. This I accepted, and was received in a like flattering manner, being at the same time introduced to the captains of several of their ships, and his own officers, the commodore desiring me to consider myself as much at home on board his ship at all times, as in my own, at the same time expressing himself perfectly willing to render any friendly assistance in his power, that I might stand in need of; while, in case of his absence, the same would be promptly attended to by the then commander of their fleet. I returned him many thanks for his politeness and courtesy, and shortly after returned in his barge on board the Betsey.[21]

Americans took greater pains to record the responses of Europeans to their arrival in the Pacific world than they did with the responses of the Pacific peoples themselves. Navigating between the European community to which they aspired and the "other" which provided a ploy, American journals brought into the public sphere the connection between the legitimacy of nation and the refinement of the individual. Samuel Shaw, again, saw the connection in the rituals of departure as the *Empress of China* prepared for its return to "Yankee land" in 1785, noting in his journal: "About ten days previous to our leaving Canton, Mr. Randall and I visited the respective chiefs (a ceremony not to be omitted), thanked them for their civilities, and informed them of our intended departure... . The attention paid us at all times by the Europeans, both in a national and personal respect, has been highly flattering."[22]

Implicitly referencing his identity as an *American merchant*, Shaw noted with some pride that the head of English factory has assured him, "'As soon as it was known,' said he, 'that your ship was arrived, we determined to show you every national attention.'"[23]

Expecting that his journal would become incorporated in the public record, the major made certain to repeat these rites of inclusion in his journal of his second voyage, and observed, "Respecting the intercourse between the Europeans and the Americans at Canton, it would be only to repeat . . . Nationally and personally, we have abundant reason to be satisfied."[24]

As these reports document a concern with America's place in the community of civilized nations, they suggest a construction of this imagined community that resonated with emergent concepts of middle-class gentility and refinement. Such displays had practical benefits as well, particularly for a "new people" whose vessels were engaged in expanding their commerce across unfamiliar and perhaps dangerous seas. Such was the experience of the American merchantman *Franklin* in May of 1819. Fending off an attack by Malay pirates near Sumatra, the *Franklin* was able to fall in with a British warship bound for Singapore. Such were the benefits of acceptance within the civilized community.[25]

Flowery Flag Devils

For the purposes of navigating a national identity, relationships with China provided the contrast necessary to complete the picture that filled the public sphere of American and European readers. For a "new people" sensitive to issues of acceptance and inclusion, the experience of being outsiders would be unnerving. And, yet, nowhere else in the world would Americans be treated so much as outsiders. Indeed, the world of American expatriates in Canton was, in Downs's poignant description, a "golden ghetto." Their position in China was made clear in the designation the Chinese reserved for all but their own—the *fan-qui*.[26] As the English residents, who had been there at least since the mid-1700s, would have explained it to the "new people": "Many persons may be puzzled to understand the meaning of the word FAN-QUI. Those who have been to China will comprehend it well enough, as they must often have heard it applied to themselves. It literally signifies 'barbarian wanderer' or 'outlandish demon.'"[27]

The site of resident life came to symbolize their enforced separation and isolation. Long, narrow factories or hongs, each containing a godown, or warehouse, and factory, or offices and living quarters, served as residences, entertainment sites, and warehouses.[28] Removed to the peripheries of China, pushed to the outskirts of Canton, perched along the banks of the Pearl River, theirs was a suffocatingly small world. The Emperors had dictated that the *fan-qui* should be few–there were rarely more than a dozen before 1820, frequently outnumbered by transient visitors–enclosed in a neighborhood of less than 12 acres.[29] Surrounding the compound was a tall fence and later a wall, which held the "barbarians in and apart."[30] The most interesting immediate attraction, the execution ground, was less than a mile away from the factories.[31] The design virtually ensured that the residents would see the world through the lenses of ethnic, cultural, and national identity. The layout of Canton's resident foreign community served as a visible symbol of ethnic and cultural differences, of categories of "residents" and the Eastern "other." As Major Shaw observed,

> *The limits of the Europeans are extremely confined; there being, besides the quay, only a few streets in the suburbs, occupied by trading people, which they are allowed to frequent. Europeans, after a dozen years' residence, have not seen more than what the first month presented to view. They are sometimes invited to dine with the Chinese merchants, who have houses and gardens on the opposite side of the river; but even then no new information is obtained. Every thing of a domestic nature is strictly concealed, and, though their wives, mistresses, and daughters are commonly there, none of them are ever visible.*[32]

Where those who crafted Imperial policy of enforced isolation and separation aimed to prevent outsiders from contaminating the virtues of the Celestial Empire, Americans–the "flowery flag devils"–depicted the illiberal restrictions of a decadent civilization.

Commerce, Civility, and National Character

The restrictions that circumscribed the liberty of American expatriates in Canton, elaborately detailed in their letters and journals, emerged not just because they were *fan-qui*, but also because they were merchants. They came to the Celestial Empire to engage in commerce, and commerce, as it was understood and practiced in the Early Republic, colored their representations of every aspect of Chinese society. In constructing Canton for an American audience, expatriates in Canton and throughout the Pacific made implicit reference to the distance between what they saw abroad and what they held as conduct appropriate to the community of civilized nations. For most, the experience in China was less an adventure than a sacrifice, made often in desperation, to gain a competency and entrance into the commercial community at home. As Robert Bennet Forbes described to his wife back in Boston in April 1839: "I sometimes think the ship I have taken was not justified by any state of affairs, that it was a cruel sacrifice. Then a pain comes to me & the reflection that I could only have remained home in a state of dependence, that I must have incurred obligations which could never cancel. By coming here I have done all I could to retrieve my fortunes & procure an independence."[33]

Furthermore, for a people who claimed their birthright in a struggle against commercial constraints, and for whom commerce and virtue were emerging as an intertwined marker of a nation's progress, such exclusion was inimical to the canons of national civility. Throughout the West, indeed, free commerce was becoming associated with enlightened values, particularly the concept of progress, and was increasingly understood as a means for extending the benefits of civilized living to less advantaged peoples. As Ezra Stiles predicted in a 1783 essay,

> The great American revolution, this recent political phenomenon of a new sovereignty arising among the sovereign powers of the earth, will be attended to and contemplated by all nations. Navigation will carry the American flag around the globe itself: and display the thirteen stripes and new constellation at bengal and canton, on the indus and ganges, on the whang-ho and the yang-tse-kiang; and with commerce will import the wisdom and literature of the east. . . . there shall be an universal traveling too and fro, and knowledge shall be increased. This knowledge will be brought home and treasured up in america; and being here digested and carried to the highest perfection, may reblaze back from america to europe, asia and africa, and illumine the world with truth and liberty.[34]

Echoing an expansive commercial interpretation of history was John Warren, who enthralled a Fourth of July audience in Boston in 1783 with a speech in which he promised: "The connections that may be formed by commercial intercourse, will not only be a source of wealth, and procure leisure for scientific pursuits, but a reciprocity of kind offices will expand and humanize the heart, soften the spirit of bigotry and superstition, and eradicate those rooted prejudices, that are the jaundice of the mind, the great obstacle to its improvement in knowledge and virtue, and particularly to its reception of that grace of the gospel which maketh wise to eternal life."[35]

In a culture in which business was considered an endeavor both personal and professional, national and individual, character mattered greatly. The representation of commerce as enlightened adventure resonated with the quest for national character and the maritime experiences that seemed to answer the challenge in the Early Republic. American readers would beam proudly when Alexis de Toqueville characterized their enterprise in terms of heroic achievement: "An American navigator leaves Boston to go and buy tea in China. He arrives at Canton, stays a few days there, and comes back. In less than two years he has gone around the whole globe, and only once has he seen land. Throughout a voyage of eight or ten months he has drunk brackish water and eaten salted meat; he has striven continually against the sea, disease, and boredom; but on his return he can sell tea a farthing cheaper than an English merchant can: he has attained his aim."[36]

Images of heroic commerce did not have a place within the Confucian value system that structured Chinese thought, however, and even in the bustling port of Canton such mercantile activity merited not approbation, but condemnation. As merchants, purveyors of useless goods, Chinese officials considered "them allied with the lowest and vilest orders of the people, to break through the best institutions of the country, and to deprave the morals, and thus to alienate the affections of those whom they consider their children."[37] China's mandarins, many trained in the values of a Confucian hierarchy, made every attempt to regulate and retrain the excesses of what they saw as unseemly conduct. The tensions that a rose from conflicting value systems were inevitable.

Americans saw in international commerce an opportunity to extend their republican vision to the world and to "humanize men by refining their manners and morals." Yet, this artifact of the Enlightenment would be sorely tested by the inefficiencies that characterized Canton's business practices. After dabbling in the China trade, some merchants found the labyrinth of regulations so contrary to their ideals of commercial virtue, they moved to other waters. Even a premier mercantile genius such as Elias Hasket Derby of Salem found the China trade more trouble than it was worth. As Major Shaw discovered on his first visit to the factories, Americans' expectation that they could trade freely and efficiently would be dashed on the restrictions that governed foreigners' conduct there. Most obvious were the infamous Eight Regulations established by the Imperial government to protect the Chinese from the taint of the *fan-qui*, and reissued or increased by the imperial government until the Treaty of Nanking in 1842.[38] They precluded a variety of practices common to the West and used by merchants in virtually every other port in the world. Americans learned, for instance, they were prohibited from year-round residence in Canton, and from riding in sedan chairs, owning firearms, employing Chinese servants, or loaning money to Chinese merchants. They were to be closely supervised by a merchant of the Co-hong, who would serve as intermediaries for all communication between the *fan-qui* and the imperial government. Perhaps most grievously, foreigners were not allowed to bring women to Canton.[39] Under the imperial regime, even one's movements, so necessary to the regular flow of business activity, were constrained, Shaw complained, by the requirement that "Every Chinese, excepting the co-hoang and persons in office, is obliged to have a chop for visiting the factories, which is renewed every month, and for which servants, and even coolies, hired at three dollars a month, must pay half a dollar."[40]

In Captain Edmund Fanning's 1834 travelogue, *Voyages Round the World*, American readers vicariously experienced the frustrations that an American merchant could expect to encounter in the labyrinth of Chinese regulations. In his August 1798 landing at Macao, as he told his audience, "for a commencement I was met by an unexpected difficulty, and one that at first was like to have caused a vast deal of trouble before it was removed."[41] Fanning was astonished to discover that, having earlier rescued survivors of an English wreck, he would not be allowed to carry them upriver to Canton because several of his charges were women. Despite repeated efforts, he lamented, "Nothing was sufficient to induce these officers to vary or make any allowance for a case (as this) not contemplated by their laws. Afraid of having his head taken off, the mandarin always replied, 'It no have China custom; how can, do.'"[42] Throughout the anecdote is the implication that he has entered a commercial Wonderland in which his republican vision would be "Not much enlightened, or greatly pleased with this sublime reasoning, [and] rather heavy hearted at so dark a beginning."[43] Even after the impasse was negotiated, Captain Fanning discovered that further obstacles would hamper his progress, and that only "after a series of tedious and vexatious examinations at five chop houses on the way up, I arrived in three hours time."[44] Fanning returned in September 1801 to find that the Western impetus for progress and change had had little effect on Eastern traditions, and "Every thing was moving forward as usual; the same routine, the same regulations, not an alteration or improvement to be observed: the Chinese are a peculiar people in this respect, and tenaciously adhere to old customs and forms."[45] The English physician C. Toogood Downing, who spent two decades about Canton, advised his readers that the illiberal restrictions had not loosened by 1838, although "Attempts have lately been made . . . to traffic with the natives in various inlets along the coast, but without success. Prejudice has assisted the action of the laws, in preventing all intercourse with strangers, but that allowed by the despotic government of the Celestial Empire."[46]

"The knavery of the Chinese"

The inefficiencies and bureaucratic obstacles were not all that frustrated a republican vision of free trade invigorating the world with liberal ideas. In constructing Canton for American readers, expatriate merchants portrayed a decadent world in which deceit tainted every transaction and the "real Jonathan" had to be vigilant, as "the petty dealers are not to be believed for an instant, or credited a shilling, as they are devoid of honourable principle in money matters."[47] William C. Hunter, of Russell and Company, who spent most of his life in Canton and Macao, advised that the small shopkeepers were "the greatest ruffians that can be imagined."[48] Even Major Shaw, whose responsibility it was to encourage American trade with the East, warned his readers that "The knavery of the Chinese, particularly those of the trading class, has become proverbial. . . . it is allowed that the small dealers, almost universally, are rogues, and require to be narrowly watched."

In representations of Yankee virtue in the East, the "real Jonathan," experiencing "imposition to perfection," could be outraged at the rampant corruption he perceived—and reported—throughout Chinese society.[49] The log of Thomas Ward, captaining the *Minerva* from Salem to Canton in 1809, contributed a petulant view to the American public sphere. After sounding Whampoa anchorage, he warned:

> *You will now or before perhaps have some applications for the birth of ship Comprador, and they are all without exception a set of cheats, & this they will vouch for, if you should doubt their rascality. . . . They will expect a Cumshaw of 260 or 280 dollars for the Liberty of cheating you out of twice that sum, & that too with your consent as it were, as you are knowing to the fact, without having the power to prevent it. . . . The price of every article must be named in the agreement & he bound as fast as you can bind him.*[50]

Captain Ward's distaste was exemplified in the petty officialdom of compradors and Hong merchants through which he had to work. Middlemen such as Consuiqua, for instance, epitomized the vices of the East, and Ward described him as "Rich—roguish—insinuating—polite—sends some excellent cargoes—some bad Cargoes—not attentive enough to business and a man with whom you cannot talk with safety, as he will promise everything & perform what he pleases—not to be seen always."[51] Thus, "having immersed the Ship in roguery," the "real Jonathan" who emerged in the subtext of such depictions, in contrast to the "stubborn and unfeeling mandarin," became a paragon of both commerce and virtue.[52]

What Americans perceived as corrupt behavior in the "ordinary" practice of business figured prominently in depictions of "true Yankees" in the waters of the Pacific. Piloting the mysteries of native custom and governmental regulation could be as confounding as navigating the Endeavor Straits. Chiefs, headmen, rajahs, viceroys, commanders, and mandarins displayed a myriad of unnerving ways to add time and cost to a voyage. They could be met throughout the Pacific, but the mandarins and hoppos of Canton stood out as emblems of corruption and decadence.

Against the image of a decadent rather than celestial empire, American expatriates (both residents and mariners) could represent their enterprises as consistent with the legacy of revolutionary virtue, in which "commerce elevated and expanded the human mind."[53] In their writings, the representation of corruption throughout the bureaucracy of the Celestial Empire provided Yankee writers ample opportunity to explore interwoven themes of Oriental decadence and Yankee virtue, and "the stubborn and unfeeling mandarins, governed as they were by illiberal laws and customs," came in for particular mention.[54] For instance, when Captain Edmund Fanning wanted to view a Chinese fortress, he found, "the mandarin in command . . . who, in consideration of the small sum, or cum shaw of a Spanish dollar, not only gave permission to take our walk, but also directed the officer to show us to the fort."[55] Likewise, when Fanning described his efforts to secure passage for his shipwrecked English passengers by way of Canton, in clear violation of the Eight Regulations, he observed, "the case was finally arranged by Mr. Hall, who made the mandarin a handsome cum shaw (present) . . . After this, a chop was issued for the landing of the females."[56]

Various Stages of Decay

American expatriates expected to see virtue exemplified in their own government, and they looked for examples of virtue in the political systems of other peoples. The world's oldest civilization served another nationalist function in the popular literature that poured from the pens of Canton's American expatriates. The letters and journals that filled the public sphere with reports of the East mirrored David Osgood's 1795 summary of a decaying civilization: "arbitrary rulers . . . nourishing their luxury, pride, pomp, and glory with the tears of general misery." The pervasive dishonesty, the inefficiency of commerce, the corruption of officials, the arbitrary and baffling regulations—all could be laid at the doorstep of the Imperial government. Here was an object lesson for the Early Republic: governments that failed to heed the needs of the people would eventually corrupt and erode even the highest civilization.

With Canton's execution grounds less than a mile from the factories, they could send ample evidence to American readers.[57] Even in the closing days of the American China trade, in 1844, Fletcher Webster would describe for Caleb Cushing viewing the heads of decapitated criminals "in various stages of decay."[58] Other expatriates reported execution by dismemberment and strangulation.[59] American audiences became familiar with the cangue, the "broad wooden collar that locked around the neck," preventing a prisoner's hands from touching the head, and often resulting in death by starvation or thirst.[60]

It was unlikely that Canton's expatriates could have avoided such parades of state power, particularly when the imperial authorities were determined to demonstrate a point. Often, the Western community itself was the target. One could feel it in the mandarins' frequent reminders that in this full world republican ideas of individual liberty had no place. Major Shaw alerted his readers to the dangers of a decadent civilization in the journal of his first visit, observing that here, "the Europeans, as has been noticed, are exceedingly straitened in their limits, and the Chinese let slip no opportunities of laying new impositions."[61] In describing the extravagant measures imposed by imperial authorities—"The mandarins on the quay are very vigilant, and every servant in the factories is a spy"—Canton's expatriate community reported on a society that grated against republican sensibilities, just as they positioned the image of an oppressed, decaying civilization as a marker of their own status with the community of civilized peoples.[62]

Nor were the expatriates themselves immune from what they described as the excesses of an arbitrary and brutal government. Two incidents, in particular, stood out to trace the boundaries of the community of civilized nations. Four years previous to the arrival of the *Empress of China*, as Shaw reported, two shipmates on a European vessel anchored at Whampoa *had a scuffle, in which [one of them] was killed; whereupon the Chinese demanded that the [other] should be given up. On being told that what the man had done was agreeable to the law of self-defence, they replied that they understood the matter very well, but that they must examine him before their tribunal, it being indispensable that they should take cognizance of such cases, and that after examination he should be restored unhurt. The poor fellow, upon these assurances, was delivered to the Chinese, who the next morning brought him to the waterside, in the neighborhood of the factories, and there strangled him.*[63]

More egregious still was the fate of a gunner on the British vessel *Lady Hughes*, an incident initiated during the *Empress of China*'s first visit to Canton. In firing off a cannon in salute, the unfortunate sailor had inadvertently killed Chinese citizens, and the mandarins demanded he be turned over to them. As Shaw described for American readers, "after two days spent in debating the affair, the Chinese merchants and mandarins told [the British consul] that they were satisfied, and that, as the gunner had absconded, there would be no further trouble about it. Every one thought the matter finished, till experience once more convinced them that there is no trusting the Chinese. Pankekoa, the head of the co-hoang, sent for Mr. Smith [a British supercargo], as it were on business, to come to his house, where he was immediately seized by a guard and conveyed into the city."[64]

Furthermore, the Americans' conversations with the British consul underscored a position they hope they would occupy—within the community of those who "considered the rights of humanity deeply interested in the present business."[65] Outmaneuvered, the British turned over the gunner. When Shaw returned from his second voyage in 1786, Americans readers learned, "It must occasion pain to every humane mind to reflect that this poor fellow was executed by the Chinese, on the 8th of January following."[66] In constructing Canton as an object lesson for "every humane mind" in the progress of civilization, Shaw, and the captains and merchants who followed him in the China trade, used such incidents both to knit their society of disparate interests into a whole cloth of republican values and to demonstrate the inclusion of the stars and stripes among the civilized peoples.

"Macao possesses very few things which can interest a stranger, after the novelty of seeing so remote a place has worn off." Observations such as that of C.T. Downing, rife through the expatriate literature, dismiss not just the languishing Portuguese colony that guarded the Pearl River, but all of China. Even had they been free to leave the confinement of their enclave, expatriates considered it doubtful that they would have seen anything that suggested difference, or change, or advancement. One recalls the discouragement Captain Fanning expressed in his September 1801 visit, noting that with the Chinese, "Every thing was moving forward as usual; the same routine, the same regulations, not an alteration or improvement to be observed: the Chinese are a peculiar people in this respect, and tenaciously adhere to old customs and forms."[67] And, it is in this latter impression, conveyed again and again to the reading public of early America, that they could discern foundations for their legitimacy as a people of refinement and gentility. Because, *they* were changing. They were the "new people," the pioneers of a revolutionary and liberal experiment.

The contrast was made plain in the expatriates' impressions of China's technology and arms. When Captain Edmund Fanning inspected a fortress overlooking the Pearl River in August 1798, dilapidated, neglected, and useless, he reported "in it fourteen handsome brass nine pound canon, but all very uncouthly mounted; it was besides difficult to depress or elevate these pieces many degrees."[68] The fort's soldiers presented a similar image of backwardness: "their military discipline, so far as we were able to judge by the specimens shown, was very far from being the best in the world."[69] China's navy was no more daunting. In 1794, during the affair involving the unfortunate gunner of the *Lady Hughes*, Samuel Shaw described: "the ships of war, in number upwards of forty, lay opposite the factories. Indeed, these ships were not very formidable, their force consisting of two long iron pieces, carrying about a four-ounce ball, and fixed with a swivel on a four-legged stool—while their soldiers were armed with swords, bows and arrows, and match-lock muskets, fixed with a triangle. From all I could observe of this naval parade of the Chinese, I am certain that three

European long-boats, properly equipped, might have forced their way through them, had they been five times as numerous."[70]

American mariners and expatriates frequently reminded their readers that the South China Sea was infested with pirates, and China's navy incapable of effective action. Not until a Portuguese fleet brought their guns to bear were the pirates incapacitated, for which the Europeans were rewarded with Macao.[71] As in their commercial affairs, so here, also, American visitors described a resistance to progress that would, it was predicted, ultimately leave a decadent country outside the scope of the civilized peoples. As Major Shaw reflected on the growing chasm between the peoples of the East and the West: "After the detail, in my former journal, of such matters as occur among the Chinese at Canton, there can be nothing to remark, in a second voyage, respecting a people whose manners and customs may be considered like the laws of the ancient Medes and Persians, which altered not. Consequently, any observations, on occasions succeeding a first visit, must be mainly confined to the foreign commerce."[72]

CONCLUSION

"We have laid the foundations of a new empire, which promises to enlarge itself to vast dimensions, and to give happiness to a great continent. It is now our turn to figure on the face of the earth, and in the annals of the world." So boasted the historian of the recent Revolution, Dr. David Ramsey, in his lecture, *An Oration on the Advantages of American Independence* in 1778.[73] That it was the Americans' turn to "figure . . . in the annals of the world" was a fact made clear only after several decades of encounter with other peoples. And, it is in the context of this preoccupation with their place on a global stage that we can better appreciate such treatments of American encounters in the Pacific, including Samuel Shaw's careful description of the Macao dinner party. It was both in the genteel and polite recognition they received from Europeans and in comparison to China—to the "foolish prejudices" and "illiberal laws and customs"of "these bigoted people," "this eccentric people," "this singular people," "those people"—that an American identity came to fruition.[74] As Archibald Robbins, an American sailor who spent years in another part of the Eastern world, would observe in 1831: "Although Africa holds the third rank in point of size among the four great continents that constitute our globe, in a moral, political, and commercial point of view, it is decidedly inferior to them all. While the continents of Europe and America have been making rapid progress in civilization, the arts and sciences, Asia may be said to have been, for the most part, stationary, and Africa retro-grading."[75]

In carrying commerce to the Pacific, then, American expatriates would have the opportunity to contribute also to fulfill a less mate-rial, but no less pressing, need. Their "discovery" of markets in the Pacific and Indian Oceans following the Revolution launched a buoyant celebration of American character. Through their tales of adventure in the "new lands" of the East, these author/sea captains created a literature of maritime discovery that contributed to the development of a nascent national character—the "real Jonathan" or "true Yankee."

Philadelphia's Arch Street Ferry Landing, ca. 1800, engraved by William Birch & Son. (Courtesy Library of Congress)

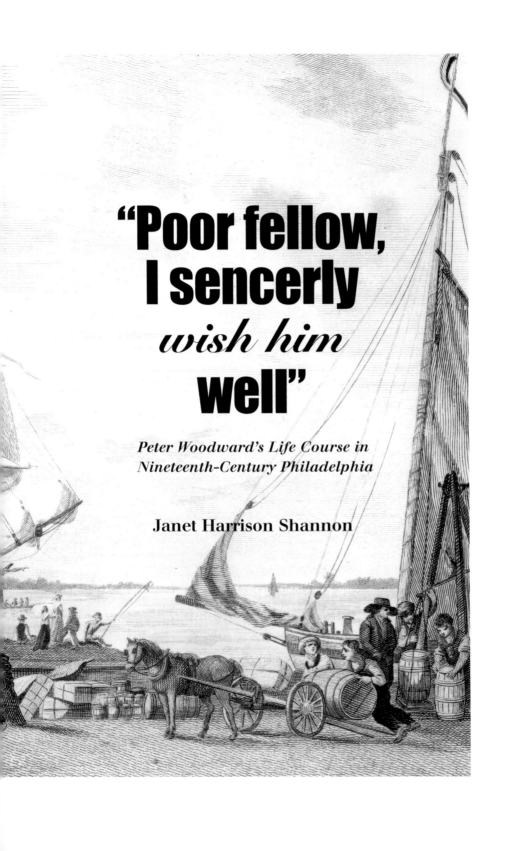

"Poor fellow, I sencerly *wish him* well"

Peter Woodward's Life Course in
Nineteenth-Century Philadelphia

Janet Harrison Shannon

People within a particular stratum share similar life chances or probabilities of benefitting or suffering from the opportunities or disadvantages their society offers.[1]

Life chances are advantages and disadvantages one can expect based upon his or her status. The concept of life course, as used by Elder et al., "refers to age graded patterns in society." It "evolves over a relatively long span as implied by the concept of a trajectory of work, earning, or marriage and also over a short time in social transitions" such as leaving home, getting and leaving a job, and, as in this case, going to sea.[2] One's life course is not merely a consequence of race, ethnicity, gender, or age, but it is also social because "its length, stages, challenges, and opportunities depend very much on the society" and the time in which one lives.[3] Using the life course perspective allows an individual to be followed from birth to death while also emphasizing "the impact of historical and societal" forces.[4] My analysis of the life course of one African American male from birth to adulthood, from 1784 to 1807, is guided by this perspective and sheds light on the impact of race, ethnicity, and power on his life chances and life course.

Not much is known about the first ten years of Peter Woodward's life. This is indeed unfortunate because childhood is the "point in history in which we live, as well as our social location."[5] And, although a child's biological characteristics are universal "his...social experiences are not." What we do know we learn from the published diary of Elizabeth Drinker.[6] Drinker's account stated that Peter was born to Alice and Anthony Woodward on March 17, 1784, probably in Kent County, Delaware.[7] At the age of two, he was separated from his parents. Left in the care of an aunt and uncle, he eventually made the journey to Philadelphia. At a charge of fifteen pounds, Warner Mifflin, a white Quaker, sent Peter to the city of Philadelphia to the home of Quakers Elizabeth and Henry Drinker. Although Peter was not the only black child who was sent to the Drinkers, he is the one written about most frequently by Elizabeth Drinker.[8] She writes not only of what happens to all children, but also her sentiments about black children in her home in 1794: "One of our daughters is to have one of the three little blacks that has [sic] lately come under our care. I feel much for the poor little fellows."[9]

Peter arrived at the Port of Philadelphia on December 6, 1794, after more than a week at sea. Once at the Drinker home, the ten-year-old was scrupulously cleaned, his hair was shampooed with a mixture of rum and larkspur, and he was given another child's clothing to wear. Although Peter had not seen his parents for eight years, four days after his arrival in Philadelphia, his father went to the Drinkers and took him to see his mother. Peter remained with his parents for several days, and on December 15, his mother returned him to the Drinkers where he soon settled into a schedule of domestic work.

Delivering messages, inquiring as to the residents' health, cleaning, washing dishes, removing ashes, attending to smaller white children, "getting in the hay" at the Drinkers' country estate, and moving items were some of young Peter's duties. Although he eventually learned to read and write, there is never any mention of his using those skills in Henry Drinker's merchant house. However, Peter did become familiar with the operation of another of Henry Drinker's business enterprises, shipping. While loading cargo at the docks, Peter fell into the hold of a vessel. He was treated immediately with a compress of Steers Opodeldoc, while blood-letting and castor oil were prescribed the next day. Peter experienced the usual illnesses and was attended by paid nurses,[10] Elizabeth Drinker, and/or Dr. Benjamin Rush.[11] Treatment for pleurisy consisted of bleeding, purging, fever powders, and a poultice. On another occasion, for an upset stomach as a result of too many blueberries, a dose of catnip tea was administered immediately, and a purge in the morning. Peter responded to the remedies and became a valued servant. Throughout his childhood, although living in the Drinker household, Peter visited with his family—mother, father, sister and brother—but, the majority of his time was spent with his family of occupation, the Drinkers.

It was almost certainly because the Drinkers kept a good household and were wealthy and influential in Philadelphia that Anthony and Alice Woodward formally bound their 12-year-old son to Henry Drinker on March 30, 1796, two years after his arrival in Philadelphia. The term of the indenture was nine years, until 1805, when Peter would be 21 years old.[12] Indeed, from 1784 to 1796,

29

Peter's young life was an uncertain one: in a 12-year period, his life course had included the trajectory of leaving home, moving to a large city, working, and being indentured.

Indenture, among other things, promoted the existence of children as wage earners, legally sanctioned their removal from the household, and caused their early entry into the labor force. In the city and county of Philadelphia these formal contracts were entered into under the auspices of one of several agencies.[13] Henry Drinker was an active member in most of these organizations, thereby allowing him direct and indirect access to the cheap labor of a number of black and white children and adults. An examination of the historical records might lead one to conclude that children under the age of 15 were sought after as servants more than older children because bound servants age 15 to 50 were taxed, whereas those under the age of 15 were not.[14] However, as Michael Grossberg argues: "Poor-law indentures, especially for blacks, resembled involuntary servitude."[15]

From 1779 until 1785, as a result of the Gradual Emancipation Act of 1780 and the influx of African Americans from the Upper South, the number of indentures in Philadelphia rapidly increased.[16] Once in Philadelphia, persons were indentured as servants, or in other menial occupations, for a specified period of time, usually until the age of twenty-one.[17]

In considering Peter's adolescence, which covered the years 1796 to 1801, several things occurred in Philadelphia that would have had special meaning for him: the increase in the black population, the increase in voluntary associations, and the increase in black churches. He would have become aware of the duality of his existence by noticing the differences between him and white children and the differences in the black and white families and communities. For Peter, more personally and intimately, he also experienced the physical development of primary and secondary sexual characteristics and his own rapid growth and weight increase.

As he aged, his household duties changed and he took on more responsible positions, but they were always unskilled and always related to the Drinker household and its occupants. When Henry Drinker was away from the home, as he was on many occasions, Peter slept in the passage to guard the house. At the age of 19, he was made a hostler.[18] We know he was a good servant because Elizabeth never wrote that he was troublesome, nor was he sent away to jail or to other households as some of the other children had been.[19]

On March 20, 1805, Peter was free, "if," as Elizabeth wrote, "being 21 years of age and [out] of his time will make him so."[20] There was no reference to a celebration of his freedom nor were immediate plans made regarding his freedom. There was "no talk of parting yet."[21] Elizabeth wrote only, "poor fellow I sencerly wish him well."[22] Her poignant phrases indicate Peter's lot as a free black man, an unindentured young man with no special training. Young adulthood, for Peter, signaled by his emancipation, indicated that he was free of his obligation to the Drinkers and that he could do, more or less, as he wished. However, although he was free to travel, there was still the possibility that he could be seized and sold into slavery. Possibly because of this threat and other reasons, leaving his family of occupation was not easy for Woodward and it is through Elizabeth Drinker's writing that we see what he encountered as he attempted to separate himself physically and emotionally from the Drinkers. Leaving their employ would reduce his dependence on them for financial and emotional support. He would no longer be under their authority. He would become a black man making his way in a white, male world. We can follow this stage of his life course only to 1807–the age of 23.

In spite of being "out of his time," Peter continued to work for the Drinkers. On November 20, 1805, perhaps overly confident of his new status and aware of his domestic responsibilities, he had an altercation with a neighbor, named Cake, a hatter. Cake routinely put his trash on the Drinker property and Peter usually disposed of it. One day, Peter put the trash back on Cake's property. Cake struck Peter severely and Peter retaliated. Warrants were issued and both parties appeared before a magistrate. In the process Henry Drinker admonished Cake that he should have come to him with his complaint instead of physically attacking Peter.[23]

With a change in status came a desire for change in other aspects of his life–especially employment. Undoubtedly Peter grew tired of the usual domestic chores and the few jobs that were available to him in the city and county of Philadelphia. Other than being a servant or a laborer, sawyer, ragman, or bone picker, there were limited opportunities for black males. For this reason, the sea attracted a large number of black men. In fact, one quarter of the black male population of Philadelphia worked as mariners. One seaman indicated: "To drive carriage, carry a market basket after the boss, and brush his boots, or saw wood and run errands, was as high as a colored man could rise."[24]

Although seafaring was a dangerous calling, the pay was good and blacks received the same compensation as whites for the same work. These factors offered men afloat a degree of equality not available on land. In addition, there was a demand for crewmen during this time. Indeed, Peter was in the right place at the right time, for the Port of Philadelphia was an active one and much of this activity involved Philadelphia's lucrative trade with Cuba.[25] Moreover, Peter had sailed on the Delaware from Kent County to Philadelphia and probably many times from Philadelphia to New Jersey with and for the Drinkers. He had also worked for Henry Drinker on the docks loading cargo; therefore, a sea voyage was something he would have considered seriously. Additionally, tales of foreign places, especially of Haiti and Cuba where people of African descent were in the majority, might have held a special allure for Woodward. Or, perhaps, it was a desire for continuous employment and a regular monthly salary of at least $16.00 that compelled him to try the seafaring life. All of these reasons and more might have crystallized for him at this stage in his life, when he had been free for less than a year.

On January 11, 1806, 21-year-old Peter Woodward applied for and received his seaman's protection certificate.[26] Henry Drinker accompanied him as he sought the necessary documentation and witnessed his signature, probably also attesting to the facts and his good character. "Peter," Elizabeth noted, "has got from C.[lement] Biddle what is called a protection, I wish it may prove one."[27] Despite Elizabeth's protestations, Woodward announced he was going to sea. She confided in her diary:

> *Our Peter Woodward made up his mind to go a voyage to sea, and has engaged to go in a sloop belonging to Cope and Thomas, to St. Domingo. A Son of John Thomas and another of Henry Drinker junr. are going in the same Vessel as Supercargos: We knew not of Peters intention 'till he had engaged himself: We have said all that is proper to discourage him, laying before him the risks he will run, not only in winters passage, but the danger of his being taken and made a slave*

of, being black, but all will not do, he has long wished to go to sea; poor fellow![28]

That John Thomas's son and the Drinkers' nephew went on the same voyage as supercargoes, while Peter traveled as a member of the crew, is indicative of his life chances as a free black man.[29] Notwithstanding the dangers associated with a sea voyage, that he pursued this course not only confirms the limited employment opportunities available to him in the city of Philadelphia but sheds light on the biological and social sequence of his birth, childhood, and maturity. Even though literate, the opportunity of being a supercargo was not afforded him. Clearly, society at that time held many disadvantages for young, black men. These realities explain Martha Putney's claim that in 1804, 908 blacks shipped out of Philadelphia.[30]

Elizabeth Drinker's strong opposition to the voyage appears to have been more than her concern over the loss of a valued servant. She wrote about his going to sea a great deal, expressing worries similar to those of a mother over a child's departure on a hazardous trip. However, nothing could dissuade Peter from sailing, and he set about selling his prized possessions and preparing for his journey. Thus, we see another transition for Peter caused by the unique social, historical, and economic events of his period.

The January 13th sailing date was postponed because the ship filled with water and sank. While waiting for another vessel, Peter continued working at the Drinkers and one evening worked as a waiter. On February 5, 1806, Peter announced that he was leaving the next day and would sail shortly. Elizabeth's worried: "James Wood says that if the French takes them, Peter being a Negro, … they will hang him, the idea has given me pain, to tell him such a thought just now, as he seems determined, would be hard perhaps, yet I hardly know how to forbare."[31] Peter, dressed in a sailor's outfit, disregarding all admonitions, and with the promise of $16 a month in wages, left the Drinker house.

The ship was to sail on the 9th at nine o'clock in the morning. Peter returned to the Drinkers on the eighth to bid them farewell. Henry cautioned him, "to keep clear of strong drink and profane language," echoing advice that Elizabeth had offered previously in addition to other appropriate warnings she "thought necessary."[32] He took a chest with him aboard the "small old vessel," *The Rising*

Sun, which was bound for Santiago de Cuba. Unfortunately, an unfavorable wind on the 9th caused a further delay and Peter visited the Drinkers twice that day.

Finally, on the 10th of February, Woodward's vessel cleared the port of Philadelphia. The crew list, dated that day, indicates that Peter Woodward, "a native of Kent County in the state of Delaware, a free black man," sailed out of Philadelphia on the sloop *The Rising Sun* of Philadelphia bound for Santiago de Cuba. The master of the vessel was Jacob Sulger with a crew of six.[33] Peter was not physically the smallest, nor the youngest; however, he was the only person of color onboard. Physically he was described as aged 21, 5 feet 6 inches in height, with "black woolly" hair and "square built" with a scar on his right arm.[34]

On April 2, Elizabeth received a letter from Peter that stated that the voyage had not been as bad as anticipated. Woodward reported that he had been seasick only once. He expected to return to Philadelphia in April or May. On April 9, 1806, *Poulson's American Daily* reported that *The Rising Sun* had arrived at Cape Français.

Recording all the news of *The Rising Sun* in her diary, Elizabeth's continued concern is evident when the old sloop returned to its home port and docked at the Lazaretto.[35] Having not seen Peter as soon as expected, she assumed he remained at the Cape with the supercargoes. Happily, on July 15, she wrote: "Our Peter Woodward came this Afternoon, he is well, and if he can get a good place wishes to stay on Shore, if not he will go to sea again."[36] This provocative entry indicates the dilemma the 22-year-old faced and informs us that the sea voyage might not have been an altogether positive one. If Woodward chose to remain there his options were somewhat limited.

John Moore, who worked for Jacob Downing, had replaced Peter at the Drinkers.[37] According to Elizabeth, because John had performed satisfactorily, "it would not do to turn him off."[38] This entry is revealing because in spite of having known Peter for nearly 12 years, her sincere concern for his condition while at sea, and her realization of the hazards of the sea, he was not re-hired upon his return. Perhaps the Drinkers thought that Peter might leave again to go to sea and having a reliable servant was more important than employing an adventurous young man, however well known. Peter did perform various jobs for them, but it is clear that there was not enough work for him to do, and therefore not a sufficient amount of pay. Because of the scarcity of work with the Drinkers, Peter worked for Manuel Eyres[39] in Kensingtown District for the month of June.

Although no longer working for the Drinkers nor living in their house, Peter remained in close contact with them. On September 1, he took them a dozen birds that he had shot. An entry in Elizabeth Drinker's diary dated September 23, 1806, confirmed her ongoing concern about him; she wrote, "Our Peter, a foolish Blockhead, is married on first Day last, to a girl of Hazelhursts, who is not free—and by accounts not so good as she ought to be—I am sorry for Peter!"[40] This telling entry sheds light on the indenture system: "not free" meant that Peter's betrothed was still indentured and, according to Elizabeth, not of good character. Indeed, her disappointment in the marriage is apparent because she never mentions Peter's wife's name. There was no offer to host a wedding supper, as she had proposed to do for other servants, nor does she record any specifics of the nuptials.

As 1806 ended with Peter experiencing a change in his life course, so 1807 brought still more changes. In addition to being a married man, his employment was still irregular. At some point, he went to work for John Hearts. In March of that year, Peter's father died "of a cramp in his stomach." That morning his father's second wife went to the Drinker house "for a shirt to lay him out in." Elizabeth sympathized, "poor old Anthony! I believe he was a sufferer in some respects."[41] Thus, over the years Woodward's family situation changed significantly: from leaving the care of an aunt and uncle, to moving in with and working for the Drinkers, freedom, a sea voyage, and the deaths of his sister and parents.

No doubt, his father's death caused Peter to consider his own mortality and that of his family. Hard choices and difficult decisions would have to be made, and he sought the advice of those who had been a part of his life for so many years. Even though free, out of his time, hiring his own time, and married, Peter sought not only Henry Drinker's advice, but also his help in finding a job. As Elizabeth Drinker indicated, the master/servant relationship was still maintained: "Peter Woodward came this evening to talk with his Master and JD. he seems inclined to go to Atsion to work there, as he is about leaving John Hearts service."[42] As a result of their conversation, Peter did leave Hearts' employ, and he and his wife moved to Atsion, New Jersey.[43] In this move, too, Peter was dependent upon the Drinkers for his livelihood—Henry Drinker and his son-in-law Jacob Downing owned the foundry at Atsion.

A few weeks after Peter left Philadelphia, a note was delivered to Elizabeth from the manager of the ironworks in Atsion, stating that the couple "behave well, and are very serviceable and handy."[44] Elizabeth was "pleased to hear it."[45] It is unclear whether they worked in the foundry or the household. The words, "serviceable and handy," imply that the Woodwards were servants in the household. What is clear, however, is that in Atsion, Peter and his new wife found a flourishing town, with several shops, mills, and a post office, as well as friends and relatives from Philadelphia, thus beginning the cycle of their married life. The diary entry concerning 23-year-old Peter was made on November 17, 1807. Elizabeth made one more entry before her death, a week later, on November 24. The significance here is that one who had spent so much of his life with Elizabeth Drinker would be mentioned so very close to the end of her days. Her death surely signaled the closing of a door on a part of Peter's life and the opening of another. However, we are not privy to the details of that life at this time.

Had Elizabeth lived, no doubt we would know more about the life of Peter Woodward. Therefore any conclusions are merely speculative: Peter Woodward and his wife might have remained in Atsion, New Jersey, where there were a number of foundries. For extra money, they might have done whitewashing or worked in the cranberry bogs. Or not being able to support his family, Peter might have returned to the sea. However, from 1809 through 1813 the number of departures from the port of Philadelphia declined because of British interference. According to Salvucci, after the War of 1812 sailings from Philadelphia to Cuba increased. This prosperity continued into the 1820s.[46]

Woodward's wife might have done domestic work in the household of others, depending upon the terms of her indenture. Certainly we can assume that Peter was never in a position to earn enough income so that his wife could remain in their home, doing only "her own work." Any male children born of the union probably would have worked in the foundry as laborers, or in homes as servants. Female children would have worked in the home of others as their parents had done. It is safe to assume that they would have been indentured and might have been sent to Philadelphia. Finally, we know that the Woodwards would have kept in contact with their relatives in Philadelphia and elsewhere and would have established a system of friendship and kinship with other blacks in New Jersey.

Tracing the life course of individual African Americans is difficult because of the paucity of the historical record. However, the sparse information that we have been able to gather about the life course of one individual is encouraging. A certain young man who was indentured has been followed from childhood through early adulthood. If similar information can be found for others for whom indenture contracts exist, it will be possible to delineate in great detail the life course available to a growing number of African Americans during the nineteenth century.

The USS *Wabash* (right) and USS *Constellation* of the Mediterranean Squadron lie at anchor off Naples, ca. 1858, in this painting by Tomaso de Simone. (Mystic Seaport 1989.105.20)

"No Common Lot":

An African-American Sailor's Half-Century at Sea
in the
Age of Sail

Julie Winch

A casual observer walking along Philadelphia's Front Street on a steamy day in July of 1810 might well have paused to stare at two individuals making their way to Alderman Alexander Tod's office.[1] Both were African Americans, one a tall, striking-looking man in his mid-40s, and the other a boy of ten or eleven. If our hypothetical observer were himself a member of the city's sizable black community, or if he were a white merchant or artisan, he might well have recognized the man. James Forten was most definitely a personality. A veteran of the Revolutionary War, a highly successful sailmaker, the owner of various rental properties, a past Grand Master of the African Masonic Lodge, a powerful voice on the vestry of St. Thomas's African Episcopal Church, James Forten was a man of distinction whose worth was acknowledged by many in the city.[2]

But who was the child walking by his side? A son perhaps? There was a certain family resemblance. But anyone who knew much about James Forten knew that as yet he had no son. An apprentice? Forten had made a concerted effort to create an integrated workforce. A white man had given him his start in business, and he was determined to train anyone, white or black, who applied to him for work and appeared intelligent and industrious. His sail loft was noted for its harmony, its productivity, and (perhaps the factor that made it so successful) its sobriety.[3] But the young lad marching along Front Street with James Forten was neither his son nor his apprentice. In fact, he was his nephew and his namesake, James Forten Dunbar.

James Forten Dunbar was a remarkable character in his own right, yet he was also one of those individuals who falls so easily into that category of faceless people whose histories are seldom written. He was black and he was poor. He was also a sailor, and sailors, irrespective of race, generally escaped the attention of census-takers, publishers of city directories, and compilers of other sorts of records. They were seldom ashore to be counted. They generally did not own much property and relatively few of them wrote wills. In short, they did not leave the kind of paper trail a historian normally looks for. However, there *are* records one can turn to. The life of James Forten Dunbar is written not in the censuses and city directories so much as in the records of the vessels on which he served. His story is bound up with theirs. For half a century he sailed the world's oceans in the merchant marine and then in the

United States Navy. On that hot and humid day in July of 1810, when our hypothetical observer chanced upon him, his uncle was taking him to Alderman Tod to launch him on his career at sea.

To get a sense of James Forten Dunbar's long career as a seafarer, we need to begin by looking in greater detail at his background. What prompted him and his friends to think that the sea might provide him with a living? As a free person of color in the new American republic, what were the expectations and opportunities that would help set his life's course?

James Forten Dunbar was a representative of the fifth generation of Fortens born in Philadelphia and the third generation to enjoy legal freedom. His great-great-grandfather, a West African whose name is lost to us, was brought to the infant colony of Pennsylvania in the early 1680s, soon after William Penn's own arrival. He lived out his life as a slave, and his son was born into bondage in the city that was rapidly emerging as one of the major centers of commerce in the British empire. That man, whose name is also unknown, secured his freedom, probably through self-purchase. He married a free woman of color, and their children, Thomas and Ann Elizabeth, were free from birth in a time and place where the vast majority of African Americans were slaves. Both children prospered. Thomas turned to the city's flourishing shipyards and managed to find work as a sailmaker. He married an African-American woman named Margaret, and they had two children, Abigail, born in 1763, and James, born in 1766.[4] Abigail should have been a heiress in a modest way, for Ann Elizabeth, a shrewd woman of business, left her enough for a decent dowry, but a series of disasters overtook the family. Thomas died unexpectedly in late 1773 or early 1774, and then the Revolutionary War broke out. At age 14, James Forten enlisted on board a privateer and was reported killed during an engagement with the enemy. However, the family's prospects picked up with the war's end. To the joy of his mother and sister, James reappeared. The reports of his death had been exaggerated, although he had come close to death in the months he spent as a prisoner of the British.[5]

As the war with Britain drew to a close, Pennsylvania's lawmakers moved to outlaw slavery. True, little was said of civil and political rights for free people of color, but the Fortens knew that the ending of slavery must inevitably benefit them, freeing them from the dangers of being kidnapped into slavery, a fate that sometimes befell unwary or unlucky freeborn men and women. A network of black schools, churches, Masonic lodges, and self-improvement societies sprang up in Philadelphia as African Americans from all over the new United States, some legally free and others slaves fleeing their owners, flocked to the city.[6] One man of color who found Philadelphia very much to his liking was sailor William Dunbar. Arriving from who knows where, he soon found work in the bustling port city. And then he met Abigail Forten. The two were married on April 10, 1784 at St. Paul's Episcopal Church.[7]

Almost immediately, William Dunbar set sail for England on merchant Thomas Truxtun's ship, the *Commerce*. He persuaded his new brother-in-law, James Forten, to ship out with him—or perhaps Abigail sent her brother along to keep an eye on her husband. William Dunbar's goal seems to have been to earn money to help support a family.[8] Young James Forten, on the other hand, went to sea in search of adventure. He stayed a full year in England, while Dunbar headed right back to Abigail. That would be the pattern of the couple's 21 years of marriage. William shipped out regularly while Abigail cared for their growing family and probably did domestic work to supplement the household's income. Abigail and William had four children who survived to adulthood: Margaret, born in 1785; Nicholas, born in 1786; William Jr., born in 1792; and James, born on July 1, 1799.[9]

It is not surprising that William and Abigail Dunbar should have named their youngest child after his uncle. Again and again over the years, James Forten came to their aid. After his return from England in 1785, Forten became an apprentice in the sail loft of white sailmaker Robert Bridges. Over the next 13 years he graduated from apprentice to foreman to junior partner. With Bridges's help, he bought a home in Southwark, Philadelphia's dockyard area, and he shared that home with his elderly mother and the Dunbars. He began investing in rental properties and making small loans at interest. He had a flair for business, coupled with a strong sense of commitment to his extended family. Not only did the Dunbars find shelter under his roof, but he helped them when William was at sea or without a berth. Having been to sea himself, and having many friends along the waterfront, he knew how meager a sailor's pay was. By 1799, when James Forten Dunbar was born, his uncle had become sole owner of the sail loft when Robert Bridges retired. As yet unmarried and without children, he might well be expected to take his young nephew and namesake under his wing.[10]

In February of 1805 disaster struck the Dunbar household. William left for a voyage from which he never returned. Word soon reached Abigail that he had died in the New York Hospital.[11] Without help from her brother, she and her children would be destitute. James Forten set to work to do what he could for the Dunbars. His niece, Margaret, was soon provided for. Some months after her father's death, she married George Lewis, a young African American from Delaware who was working as a journeyman in James Forten's sail loft.[12]

James Forten offered to take on nephew Nicholas as an apprentice. Nicholas accepted the invitation, but the young man disappointed his uncle and ultimately shamed the family. He spent a few years learning the elements of the sailmaker's trade before abandoning the sail loft to go to sea. He eventually jumped ship in St. Croix in 1816 and was never heard of again. He left behind a wife and several children—more mouths for Uncle James to feed.[13]

Nicholas's younger brother, William Dunbar Jr., was a much worthier recipient of his uncle's generosity. In time he, too, went to sea, but only after he had truly mastered the sailmaker's trade. His skill with needle and canvas enhanced his value to the various captains he served under. He regularly shipped out as a sailmaker, with better pay and a higher status than the ordinary seamen.[14]

And what of James Forten Dunbar? The baby of the family, only five when his father died, he was allowed to remain with his mother for some years, but eventually his uncle decided it was time for him to be settled respectably. And that was what prompted the visit to Alderman Tod in the summer of 1810. James was to get his seaman's protection papers and be sent off to sea.

Getting one's papers was essential for anyone embarking on a voyage as a crew member. The practice of issuing these papers had begun in the mid-1790s as a move to protect American sailors from impressment into the French or British navies. The sailor and a friend or family member went before an alderman who took down particulars: name, age, height, complexion, hair type, and so forth. The sailor was given one copy and another was filed with the

Collector of Customs of the home port. Hopefully, flourishing one's papers in the face of a foreign captain would save one from impressment, although by 1810, with the Royal Navy ever more forcefully "recruiting" on the high seas, that was doubtful. For black sailors the "protection" had an added significance. They needed to be secure from both foreign impressment and from domestic exploitation. A free black seafarer in a Southern port, or on a vessel commanded by an unscrupulous captain, was a valuable commodity to be sold into slavery if and when the opportunity arose.[15] On that July day in 1810, James Forten was trying to safeguard his young nephew from enemies both foreign and domestic. Alderman Tod took down James Forten Dunbar's particulars: a boy of 11, four feet seven inches with his shoes on, freeborn, a mulatto with black hair and black eyes, and bearing scars from the bite of a dog and a vaccination against smallpox. James Forten swore to the accuracy of the information, and young James, unable as yet to sign his name, made his mark.[16]

It is not clear if James went to sea at any point during the next few years. Certainly there is no record of his having seen service during the War of 1812. He may have made coasting voyages, the recording of which was at best haphazard, but his first overseas voyage did not come until 1819, when, shortly before his twentieth birthday, he shipped out for Liverpool on the *William Savery*.[17] Neither on shipboard or ashore was he an oddity. It is worth remembering that one in five sailors leaving the port of Philadelphia in this period was black. In fact, in virtually every American port, black sailors were a common enough sight and generally aroused little comment. As for Dunbar's destination, Liverpool was one of the world's great sailortowns, with men from every continent mingling in the waterfront taverns and boardinghouses.[18]

Sea life apparently agreed with Dunbar, or at least he saw in it opportunity. In April of 1821 he was off on a far longer voyage to Canton via Savannah on the ship *Thomas Scattergood*.[19] Had he made the voyage one year later, it would have been even more hazardous, for to the perils of the ocean would have been added the risks of enslavement. The Denmark Vesey rebellion of 1822, and rumors that African American sailors had been involved, prompted authorities in Charleston, South Carolina, to order the imprisonment of all black sailors while their ships were in port. Other ports in the Lower South, Savannah among them, enacted similar laws. As many an African American seafarer found to his cost, jailing could rapidly become enslavement. Captains were responsible for paying jail fees, and the temptation to sell a sailor into slavery was just too great for some of them to resist.[20] Significantly, after that 1821 voyage, James Forten Dunbar (so far as we know) never sailed to a Southern port during his years in the merchant marine. Not until he was in the United States Navy did he venture south of the Mason-Dixon Line.

As it was, the voyage to China was a voyage of discovery for the young Philadelphian. He spent months at sea, and then found himself in a faraway port. There all foreigners, whether black or white from the older European powers or the young American republic, were designated "barbarians" and kept at arm's length by the suspicious officials of the Celestial Empire. With his pay and perhaps a few mementoes of his travels, James Forten Dunbar returned to Philadelphia, to a young woman he had probably courted many months before and who eagerly awaited his return. On April 30, 1822, at Christ Church on Second Street, he and Mary Welsh were married.[21]

Marriage kept James Forten Dunbar much closer to home. He continued to ship out, but on much shorter voyages to Havana, a regular port of call for Philadelphia merchantmen. However, in 1825, with a newborn daughter, Abby, to provide for, he again set sail on a year-long voyage. This trip took him back to Canton with Captain William McKibbon on board the *Dorothea*. He apparently got along well with Captain McKibbon, for he sailed again with him to China the following year.[22] In 1828 Dunbar took another transatlantic voyage to Liverpool on the *Woodrop Sims*, but then there followed some years in Philadelphia living with Mary, Abby, and a young son, James Jr. The family shared a home on Washington Court with James's widowed mother. Thanks to James Forten's generosity, Abigail Dunbar, her son, and his family had the home rent-free. James Forten Dunbar worked in his uncle's sail loft and, like his brothers, plied the sailmaker's trade. His last voyage as a merchant sailor was to the East Indies aboard the schooner *Italy* in 1838.[23]

In the early 1840s the circumstances of James Forten Dunbar's life changed dramatically. In 1842 his uncle died and his Forten cousins lost control of the family business. Then James suffered a series of tragedies even closer to home. Daughter Abby died of tuberculosis in 1844. In 1846 his mother died. He may also have been widowed as Mary Welsh Dunbar simply disappeared from the records. With his family virtually wiped out—son James would die of consumption in 1848—James Forten Dunbar went back to sea, this time with the United States Navy.[24]

In October of 1846, at age 47, Dunbar joined the navy in Boston. Why he enlisted in Boston is not clear. Perhaps he had left Philadelphia on a merchantman, disembarked in Boston, and signed up there. Whatever the case, the navy recruiters were glad to receive him, and they sent him to the USS *Stromboli*. His years at sea, and his talents as a sailmaker, made him a valuable addition to a ship's company. As was the case with the merchant marine, black sailors were routinely enlisted into the United States Navy, although they could not expect to advance above the rank of able seaman.[25]

Two years later, probably just discharged from the *Stromboli*, Dunbar reenlisted. This time he was sent to the *Constitution*. He was 48 years old, one of the oldest members of Old Ironsides's company. The Keys to Enlistment say nothing more about him, but he would have sailed to the Mediterranean for what turned out to be a remarkable cruise. In 1849, in Naples, Pope Pius IX came aboard the warship—the first time a pope had ever set foot on what was technically United States territory.[26]

James Forten Dunbar next enlisted aboard a vessel in New York City in 1851, but the records are silent regarding which ship he was assigned to. In February of 1854 he was back in New York, and he was assigned to the USS *Princeton*. The following year he was sent to the *North Carolina*, and the details of his service are clearer. He had 26 years of experience at sea, and the recruiter noted both his race and his skill as a sailmaker. He enlisted, as always, as a seaman for general service for three years.[27] Apparently the *North Carolina* was only the receiving ship. Dunbar was soon reassigned to the *Cyane* and on her he served his full three years. Honorably discharged on February 3, 1858, in Norfolk, Virginia, he signed on again the very next day. Less than a year later he was in New York, enlisting on the USS *Brooklyn*.[28]

As he aged, it was harder and harder for him to find a berth. In 1861, at the very beginning of the Civil War, he enlisted in

Philadelphia on the USS *Union* as a cook, one of the few shipboard occupations available to a man of color too old to go aloft. He lied about his age, saying he was 58 when he was in fact 62, but he was discharged within a few months. Undeterred, he enlisted once more, this time in New York, in early 1862. He was assigned to the *Massachusetts* and then to the *Lacawanna.*[29] With the Civil War raging at sea as well as on land, the United States Navy was in need of experienced sailors, and Dunbar tried to use that fact to his advantage. He enlisted once more in June of 1863 as a cook and a sailmaker, probably hoping his skills and experience would outweigh his age. However, he was rejected. On July 9, 1863, James Forten Dunbar, age 65, enlisted in Boston. Over the next year and a half he served on various vessels in the South Atlantic Squadron, the *Valparaiso*, the *Wabash*, the *Daffodil* and the *Rose*. He was either discharged or deserted from the USS *Princeton* in January of 1865.[30]

Why did James Forten Dunbar continue at sea for so many years, long past the time when most sailors sought land-based occupations? To begin with, he had no one and nothing ashore. His whole life was at sea. On board ship he had food, a place to sleep, pay, and companionship. Obviously we cannot know how he spent his hours between watches or his slack time in the galley. Did he learn to read? Was he of a religious bent? Did he regale the younger men with his tales of places he had visited, people he had seen? A few things are clear. He was evidently not a fighter or a drunkard. He was never dishonorably discharged. And he spent some of his time getting tattooed. (Tattoo parlors did not yet exist. Tattooing was done on shipboard with needles and colored inks by an artistically inclined member of the crew.) On James Forten Dunbar's right arm were common symbols of the seafarer's world: a mermaid and a ship. On his left, rather poignantly, were mementoes of the people he had loved and lost: a man and a woman, and a family group.[31]

By the time the Civil War ended, James Forten Dunbar was almost 66 years old. No captain wanted him, and he had few options except the charity of his extended family or the poorhouse. He returned to Philadelphia, the city of his birth, and was admitted to the United States Naval Asylum as a "beneficiary." In the Asylum he got food, clothing, lodging, a cash allowance, tobacco, and medical care.[32] One needed a recommendation to get into the Naval

Asylum, and probably his Forten cousins helped out. William Deas Forten, James Forten's youngest son, was emerging as a powerful figure in Republican circles. With African American men soon to be legally enfranchised, he was recognized as a political power-broker who could rally the black vote. White politicians courted him, and he may well have been able to use his influence and his friends' influence to get a place in the Naval Asylum for James Forten Dunbar.[33] Did he do this to help a family member in need, or did he, perhaps, feel that Cousin James was something of an embarrassment? Perhaps the old sailor had a habit of sitting around in the elegant parlor at the Forten home on Lombard Street, singing unexpurgated versions of sea chanties, chewing tobacco, and entertaining the unsuspecting visitor with salty tales of life in the world's sailortowns. But perhaps he never even considered living with his well-heeled cousins and asking them to support him. As a sailor with half a century of seafaring behind him, perhaps he felt more comfortable in the company of fellow sailors.

In fact, James Forten Dunbar did not adjust easily to life in the Naval Asylum. At some point he was dismissed for being "very troublesome and bad." Maybe he simply did not suffer fools gladly, or maybe he gave his opinions too freely. Perhaps with William Deas Forten's help, he was readmitted "on condition" on August 3, 1867. This time he had to conform, for he had nowhere else to go. He settled down. The Asylum's monthly musters described his character and habits as "Very Good." He died in the Asylum on November 26, 1870. The official who recorded his passing composed the following piece of doggerel:

> *There is a motto 'All things must have an end'*
> *And this old sailor opposite whose name these lines are penned*
> *Has paid the debt of nature*
> *This, as by his record verified, was no common lot*
> *Though after years of service*
> *Thrust in the earth to be forgot.*[34]

In many respects this is a fitting epitaph not to James Forten Dunbar alone but to so many of the men, of many races and many nationalities, who served in the merchant marine and the United States Navy during the age of sail. It was they who took American commerce to distant lands, and who helped show the flag and protect American interests on the high seas. James Forten Dunbar won no great naval victories, discovered no new lands, pioneered no new avenues of trade. In rescuing him from obscurity, we are, in a sense, rescuing not him alone but the many thousands of his mess-mates, black and white, native-born and foreign-born, whose "common lot" was low pay, harsh discipline, almost constant danger, separation from home and family, and the dubious rewards of a sailor's life.

The Steamboat *St. Paul* is shown on the Mississippi River on this postcard mailed in 1919. (Mystic Seaport 20004.52.1)

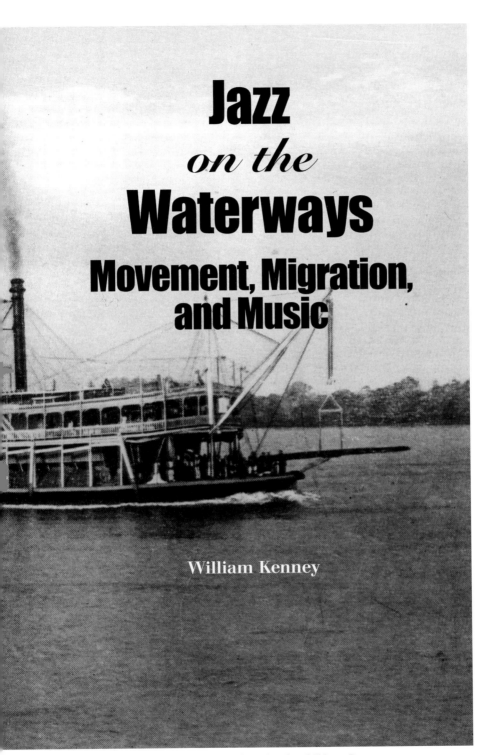

Jazz
on the
Waterways
Movement, Migration, and Music

William Kenney

In April of 1919, Louis Armstrong determined to see where his burgeoning talent as a cornetist, singer, and entertainer would take him. He announced to friends and colleagues that he would be casting off at the foot of Canal Street in his hometown of New Orleans. Armstrong, then 18 years old, had decided to accept an exciting job offer from bandleader Fate C. Marable to play in a new dance band onboard the 300-foot-long Mississippi River steamer *St. Paul*, an excursion boat that "tramped" between St. Louis, Missouri, and St. Paul, Minnesota, during the summer months. He had not then ventured much beyond the neighborhood of his birth and had only quite recently decided to become a professional musician.[1] But thrown onto his own resources from an extremely tender age, he was prepared to embark on what turned into a life of touring the circuits, playing for tourist junkets during three seasons up and down the river. Soon he took his eloquent, fugitive music on a train north to Chicago's South Side, and then by panting flivver to New York, transatlantic steamers to Europe, and airplanes around the world. His youthful decision to work out his future on America's greatest river set into motion a lifetime of translating the music he had known while re-thinking and re-inventing himself, exploring his musical capacities, and creating new meanings from his neighborhood's music.[2]

The great jazz soloist's new bandleader, Fate C. Marable, had traveled on the river for many years, charting Armstrong's northward heading by first steaming southward on the Ohio and Mississippi Rivers from his hometown of Paducah, Kentucky. The two men's trajectories crossed in the mudsill city of New Orleans where the most famous pianist and bandleader on America's inland waterways "discovered" the young cornetist. Armstrong, like most New Orleanians in those days before the automobile and the skyscraper, had clearly heard Marable playing a steamboat calliope into the night air from the foot of Canal Street. The Kentucky musician also had been deputized by Captain John Streckfus, founder of Streckfus Steamers, Inc., to recruit the latest "hot" musical stylists who were willing and able to respond to the needs of the racially segregated boats.

Armstrong and Marable were to work together for three years, becoming the two most famous musicians to play extensively what became known as jazz on the largest Mississippi riverboats. Many other important instrumentalists followed in their wake. Those whose names still resonate–Henry "Red" Allen, Bix Biederbecke, Zutty Singleton, Johnny Dodds, Warren "Baby" Dodds, Jess Stacy, George "Pops" Foster, Jimmy Blanton, Tab Smith, Gene Sedric, Clark Terry, and Wellman Braud–followed the orders of the German-American Captain John Streckfus and his sons (Captains) Joseph, Verne, John, Roy. In return, they earned steady money while moving beyond manual labor and building the foundations for professional careers that reached beyond the racial enclaves assigned to them in America.

Starting in 1901, the German-American Streckfus family pioneered in the excursion boat business by finding something remunerative to do with the largest of the old, wooden river packets that had been built to carry a variety of material goods and a few stateroom passengers. By tearing out the staterooms, replacing them with immense, polished wooden dance floors, adding a variety of concession stands and rocking and lounge chairs, and painting the whole in brightly fresh colors, the Streckfus family ran tourist excursions, "tramping" out of any river city that could produce enough customers. Entertainment played a vital role in distracting the public from the distant and too often uninteresting vistas on the mighty Mississippi.

The music black musicians played on the rivers from 1918 to 1945 emerged from intricate and complex negotiations with Joseph Streckfus, leader of the third generation of his family's Mississippi River dynasty.[3] The grandson of Balthazar Streckfus, who had migrated in the 1840s from Germany to Edgington, Illinois, was the first son of John Streckfus, founder of Streckfus Steamers, Inc. Joseph Streckfus, a licensed steam engineer and master riverboat pilot, a model of Catholic rectitude, a philanthropist, and a prominent civic leader in St. Louis, ran a tight ship. He wanted jazz on two of his boats: the 300-foot *St. Paul* and the slightly smaller *Capitol*. He deputized Fate Marable to go find it. He told his bandleader what kind of music he wanted on board. He fired any musician who got out of line or who could not read the charts. Riverboat jazz, of which the Streckfus brothers became the self-proclaimed inventors, contained a tight, unresolved tension between its African American exponents and its German-American pilots, tension of a sort found wherever black musicians performed in Jim

Crow surroundings. The Streckfus Line liked to suggest that the words jass (and thus also jazz) had come from their boat the *J.S.*, that everyone had always pronounced "jess."

Fate's musicians also negotiated with the crowds of young people, 3,000 of whom could dance at the same time on the *St. Paul's* dance floor.[4] The musicians' skin color, New Orleans origins, and musical skills earned them instant authenticity with the young white in-crowd. Since 1910, kids in big cities like Chicago, New York, and San Francisco had launched a major new craze for social dancing. Midwesterners wanted to be part of it, too, but many of them were not used to sharing social space with African Americans, particularly stylishly dressed professionals. Some young white men tended to get testy in their presence, strutting their manliness in front of the black orchestras, as well as the ladies, occasionally picking fights. Streckfus Steamers, Inc., stationed private guards around the bandstand in case of trouble.[5] The majority of the customers only stared, gaped, and gazed at the band.

The importance of this famous era of riverboat jazz that lasted from 1918 to 1945 will be found on many levels: jazz writers have emphasized the role these riverboat jazzmen played in introducing rhythmically dynamic musical improvisations to the heartland. Actually, the Streckfus Line's jazz was often a syncopated "hot dance"-band style, arrangements written for 10 to 12 musicians who added their own improvised solos. This was a style more suggestive of Fletcher Henderson's early orchestras, than New Orleans-style polyphony.[6] This "hot dance" music was the new sound that they brought to the Mississippi River Valley, and it provided an important, overlooked precedent for the big-band era of the 1930s and 1940s. In 1916, 78 r.p.m. records had introduced the all-white Original Dixieland Jazz Band to the nation, but Marable's men brought their all-black performances "live" to heartland Americans–especially, as we shall see, young white ones, in a racially segregated but powerfully suggestive riverboat context. In 1919, whites found jazz records by white musicians everywhere and live music by black musicians in a few special places like the riverboats and Harlem's Cotton Club.

But jazz on the river was far too furtive, mobile, and dynamic to be permanently shanghaied. Music in aural traditions readily travels, and the music that people called jazz had dynamic motion within it. During the first half of the twentieth century, all sorts of Americans lived in motion, emigrating from abroad to new homes, from the country to the cities, from east to west, and most importantly for jazz, from the South northward. They inevitably left behind them much of their earlier thought and behavior but readily learned to redefine themselves in the contrasts between what they thought had been and what they were seeing and hearing around them on their journeys. Musicians on the *St. Paul* and the *Capitol* were said by whites to carry their New Orleans identities with them, playing New Orleans jazz. But their lives and their music were actually taking new shape within an immense inland maritime river system, one that stretched from New Orleans to St. Paul and from Cairo, Illinois, to Pittsburgh, Pennsylvania.[7] Jazz on the river therefore became a complex and evolving set of musical gestures, and it drew upon the creativity of a host of black musicians who lived and worked on land as well as water. Jazz may have been invented in New Orleans, but once on the Mississippi and Ohio it became like a river of music, flowing into constantly changing forms and regularly overflowing the levees built to contain it.

The music that was commercialized as "jazz" throve on many varieties of travel; so much so that its slang, like the music itself, came, over the years, to incorporate metaphors of movement. Practiced players said they had "traveled miles and miles" through the paths of song; a musically rich performance was "a trip"; fans wanted to be "moved" by the music and pleaded with the musicians, "Go, Go Go!" "send me!" Jazz's close relationship to dance brought it joy in physical movement as dancers "hoofed it," "legged it," "beat the leather," "hopped," "trotted," "shimmied," and "toddled" to the music. Perspiring scholars tried to pin jazz down but, of course, it was "in process," always becoming something new depending, in part, on where it was played, its freshness carrying a ray of hope to those able to hear it. The riverboat captains ordered that its tempi be slowed lest the music and dancing shake apart those old wooden boats.

Try as they might to structure their water-born jazz, the Streckfus brothers' excursion boat enterprise did not come to grips with the other meanings of either jazz or of the river to black musicians. Armstrong's and Marable's musical odysseys unfolded within two of the most influential movements in twentieth-century American history: the Great Migration of African Americans northward from the South and a gathering momentum in the production of black and black-influenced popular culture in the United States. Although attention to the Black Migration nearly always centers on Chicago, that massive movement of human beings surged throughout the Mississippi and Ohio River valleys, bringing jazz to the major inland maritime cities like Memphis, St. Louis, Louisville, Cincinnati, and Pittsburgh.[8] Armstrong, a thoroughly exceptional musical artist, expressed through his cornet the surging, infectious spirit of hope and excitement that struggled for control over the recurrent despair of emigrants from Mississippi, Louisiana, and Arkansas. Those of them who followed the Illinois Central Railroad and U.S. Route 61 northward along the Mississippi River to places like East St. Louis and St. Louis discovered both cities trying to gain control over what they saw as a dangerous racial tide, the one city reeling from the race riot of 1917 and the other attempting to legislate residential segregation.[9] The jazz music that Armstrong articulated on the Streckfus family's riverboats gave expression to his own, and his people's, determination to create brighter worlds of freedom and opportunity through movement and travel. Inevitably, the music became what one Chicago journalist call a "syncopated threnody," melancholy lurking within the bright polyphonies and intense rhythms.

The excursion boats–like the towns and cities around them and even many of the most famous nightclubs in the big eastern cities– remained racially segregated throughout the period. A federal court order finally mandated the racial integration of excursion boats in 1969. African American riverboat musicians in general, and Louis Armstrong in particular, performed their music of hope and freedom mainly for white audiences, although in St. Louis, at least, the Streckfus company designated one night per week when black customers were allowed to buy a ticket to ride. The boats consequently became contested semi-public spaces in which rigid maritime authority held volatile social tensions in check. In fact, the tourist experience of pre-World War II riverboats depended heavily upon this unacknowledged tension between the Great Migration of African Americans northward through the Mississippi River Valley and the river packet's traditional definition of whiteness.

Many black musicians along the Mississippi used their music to fight the Jim Crow riverboats. For example, the 1920s black St. Louis orchestra promoter Jesse J. Johnson and the East St. Louis trumpeter Charles Creath refused to give in to the Streckfus Line and promoted cruises for African Americans by African Americans on the steamers *Grey Eagle, Majestic, Pilgrim,* and *City of Cairo.* They advertised the *Pilgrim* as "The Only Steamer on the Mississippi Operated by Colored People. Concessions are also Operated By Our People. Steam Calliope, Four Spacious Decks, 1500 Chairs, 500 Rockers, 3000 jazz Lights!" Jesse Johnson even promoted Fate Marable's groups, known to history as the "house bands on the Streckfus Line," in competition with that dominant company. He did so, moreover, explicitly to fight the established pattern of segregation on the river. On May 14, 1926, Johnson promoted a cruise on the *City of Cairo.* Taking out a full-page advertisement in the *Argus,* Johnson, who was always involved in dance as well as music promotions, featured "Prof. Jesse Johnson and his Paradise Boys and Girls" demonstrating to the music of Fate Marable and His Jazz Syncopators in a Big Saturday Nite Midnight Ramble for "the Exclusive Use of Our People." The "officers on our steamer are members of our group":

> *Churches, Social Clubs, Fraternal Organizations and Labor Organizations will not have to group together to secure a date on the "City of Cairo," due to the fact that our steamer is not confined to Monday Night only but EVERY NIGHT. We feel sure that each and every one will appreciate this step forward and will cooperate individually and collectively to make this mammoth undertaking a grand success.9*

Somehow these efforts to promote music and dance in the name of racial freedom on the river repeatedly foundered in what are said to have been tragic accidents. Just as the *Grey Eagle* sank in 1918, the *Majestic* burned in 1922 and the *City of Cairo* suddenly sank during the winter of 1923. The *Pilgrim*'s draft was declared to be too deep for parts of the river, and she was towed off to Tampa, Florida, where she rotted away.[10] Ultimately, Blacks in St. Louis returned wearily to the Streckfus Line's Monday night cruises for "blacks only."

By using all-black bands, the segregated riverboats channeled black music into new worlds of white popular culture. Putting what were widely publicized as "jazz musicians" onto America's hallowed gingerbread paddlewheelers created a new tension-filled social and cultural context for both the music and the boats. Compared to the honky-tonks of New Orleans, the riverboats offered what was certainly, by New Orleans standards, a wholesome, middle-class, tourist experience in which a well-rehearsed orchestra played for fairly polite social dancing. Many of the young people who crowded onto the polished dance floor may have been unaware of it, but the white "wedding-cake" superstructures, tall smoke stacks, and immense paddle wheels of the Streckfus excursion steamers still looked like those of the nineteenth-century packets so lovingly detailed by writers like Mark Twain, Edna Ferber, and Frances Parkinson Keyes. These icons of the exotic South were celebrated from 1927 to the present in *Show Boat*, the Broadway musical based on a novel by Edna Ferber with music and lyrics by Jerome Kern and Oscar Hammerstein.[11] The largest of those old wooden vessels were floating "palaces," ornate maritime mansions whose embellished decks resembled the American Gothic style of architecture that displayed a like taste for profusions of picturesque joinery around broad and deep verandas or "piazzas."[12]

But African American musicians and jazz on the segregated excursion boats quietly affirmed other, officially unrecognized patterns of meaning that have never been represented in *Show Boat*. Though first produced in 1927 at the height of the Jazz Age, that slick and enduring entertainment has persistently stirred charges of racial prejudice. The show's use of minstrel stereotypes and its fascination with miscegenation prevented it from exploring the immense dramatic possibilities embedded in black experiences and attitudes toward life on the Mississippi and Ohio rivers.

Black ragtime and jazz, for example, brought new and important elements of professionalism and labor organization to the nineteenth-century packet tradition of black stevedores who had sung as they loaded the vessel, and when finished, further entertained the passengers.[13] The riverboat stevedores had long provided whites with a riveting glimpse of the behavior and sensibilities of a people who were normally removed by Jim Crow law and tradition from white society. The music that they had made had possessed the power to fix the passengers' attention, offering a brief reminder of the riveting power of black music in a rigidly segregated society.

As the water-born jazz musicians turned to their moving work, they began their voyages through the emerging circuits of the popular entertainment business. The music that they had conceived, organized, and produced for local dancers and revelers in Louisiana was partially absorbed into the structures and sensibilities of Tin Pan Alley songs and the commercial arrangements of them created in New York City's Brill Building and delivered directly to the boats. The meeting of "hot," improvising musicians and highly commercialized popular culture created a sensation in those floating dance halls, making them the talk of the Midwest and a solid moneymaking proposition for the Streckfus family.

The excursion steamboats of the twentieth century provided a powerful venue for jazz; they were not nightclubs, but they possessed their own elemental advantages. Whatever their old-fashioned appearance, these vessels were what their owners called "tramps," ships without a fixed home port, as rootless as a Chaplinesque jazz musician out looking for a gig. Tramping modernized the traditional associations of riverboats with floating bohemian cultures of wealthy Southern planters, northern carpetbaggers, gamblers, prostitutes, racetrack titans, and nomadic musicians. If "jazz" hadn't just been invented, the Streckfus family would have had to create it in order to inject just the right jolt of musical daring to their updated riverboat saga.

Another fact of riverboat music at the dawn of the 1920s also insured that the crowds discovered a powerfully original musical experience. The *St. Paul* was neither just another dance hall nor still another speakeasy, but the largest steamboat plying the waters of America's most legendary river system. A newspaper advertisement shouted: "One block long, 75 feet wide, 5000 passengers, Three roomy decks open on all sides, 500 rockers, 2,500 comfortable seats, 5000 electric lights, 1000 electric fans. Best dance music in the United States 1500 couples can dance on the dance floor at one time!"[14]

The musical notes, beats, and chords that the musicians shanked off the intricate wooden filigree flowed into the air over the roiling, mud-filled waters of the Mississippi and the Ohio, giving even more motion to the elements and unsettling the ways in which young

Americans experienced mud, water, and air.[15] The excursion boats attempted to recreate the dreamy reverie of what French writer Gaston Bachelard called "the swan complex" in which beautiful, white, swan-like vessels floated serenely over glassy, murmuring waters. But the murderous roiling undercurrents of the Mississippi turned the river brown with swirling silt and debris, eventually deposited as mud. So, too, the emotional complexity of black jazz unsettled nineteenth-century visions of white imperial dominance of the Mississippi and the Ohio.

Most of the young white dancers probably went away thinking that they had danced to one pretty hot dance band, but the young white musicians who were then in the vanguard of jazz experimentation on their side of segregation's divide were stunned by what they heard. Trombonist Jack Teagarden, for example, expressed it this way: one evening in 1919, he wandered with a friend down to New Orleans' Canal Street moorings. Drunk and out looking for some good music, Teagarden began to hear some that he would never forget:

> I couldn't see anything but an excursion boat gliding through the mist back to port. Then the tune was more distinct. The boat was still far off. But in the bow I could see a Negro standing in the wind, holding a trumpet high and sending out the most brilliant notes I had ever heard. It was jazz; it was what I had been hoping to hear all through the night. I don't even know if it was "Tiger Rag" or "Panama." But it was Louis Armstrong descending from the sky like a god. The ship hugged the bank as if it were driven there by the powerful trumpet beats. I stayed absolutely still, just listening, until the boat dropped anchor. It was Fate Marable's orchestra.[16]

Teagarden met Armstrong that night and performed with him often thereafter, many of those performances being memorable ones.

Whites and blacks could not fully share each other's experiences of the river. The African Americans took the voyages of pilgrims, exiles, and pioneers. Theirs were exciting explorations of the Mississippi and Ohio Valley and of the unknown territories of jazz improvisation, but also exhausting and depressing struggles against the powerful racial undercurrents of American life. Their travels were not those of tourists, and their music gained depth as a result.

For many of them, the Streckfus Steamers served as floating conservatories and a means of transportation elsewhere.

For white Americans, jazz on the river brought an unsettling excitement and danger to the age-old human experiences of travel through mud, water, and air. Jazz, whether or not they realized it, announced a modem shift in the social and cultural possibilities of the Mississippi and Ohio Rivers, of the paddlewheelers, and of the rites of passage that the two offered together.[17] Excursion boat passengers sought a separation from work-a-day, conventional life on land. They discovered a mysteriously powerful sense of gliding out of their time and place, dancing in liminal excitement to a new black music on boats redolent of nineteenth-century white dominance. In the commercial tramp steamer formula, they then returned to conventional society where the river and its water music became but a recurrent, mysterious dream. Dancing to jazz on the river had celebrated in excited movement an old boat's slow passage toward a New World. That world would prove to be deeper and more dangerous than any that they had ever imagined as they gazed at the refracted surfaces of the Mississippi and Ohio, one that they would need time, luck, and insight to fathom.

Sailing, Shipping, *and* Symbolism:

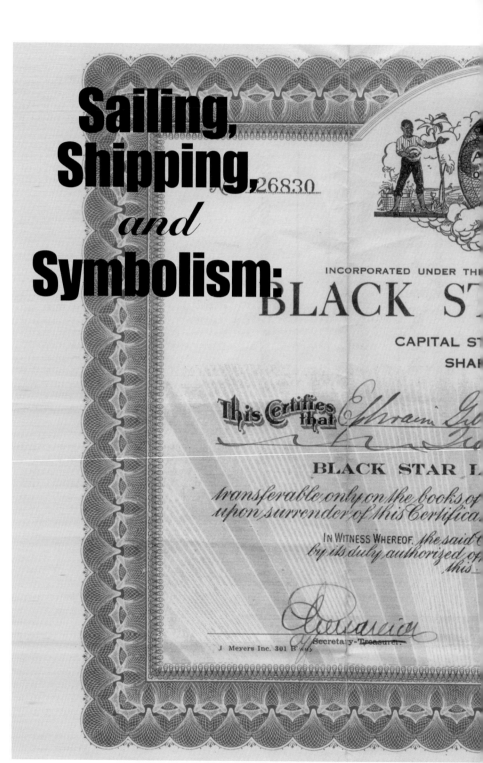

Black Star Line stock certificate, 1920.
(VFM G.W. Blunt White Library, Mystic Seaport)

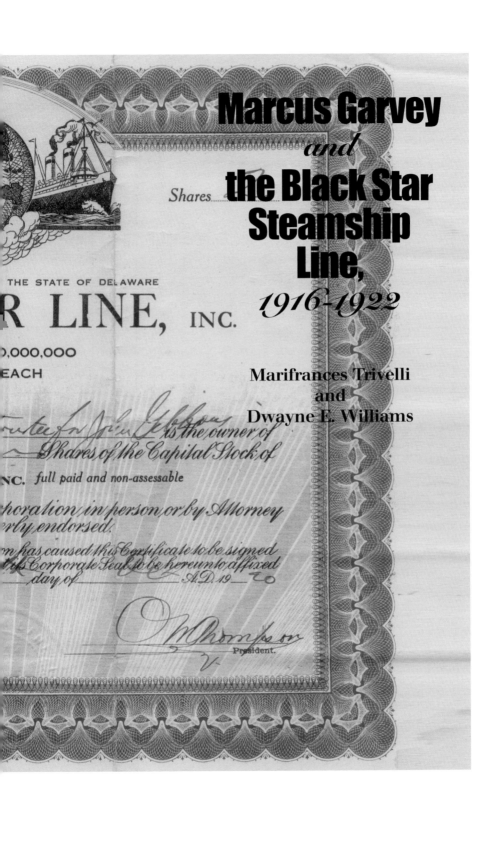

Marcus Garvey

and

the Black Star Steamship Line, *1916-1922*

Marifrances Trivelli
and
Dwayne E. Williams

Shares

THE STATE OF DELAWARE

R LINE, INC.

0,000,000

EACH

Trustee for John Gibbon is the owner of
Shares of the Capital Stock of
NC. full paid and non-assessable

poration in person, or by Attorney
rly endorsed.

m has caused this Certificate to be signed
is Corporate Seal to be hereunto affixed
day of A.D. 19

President.

Just as white men conduct a fleet of vessels called the White Star

Line, 400 million Negroes were determined to start and operate the

Black Star Line (Marcus Garvey, April 1919).

INTRODUCTION

Recent scholarship has reflected an increasing interest in the relationship between Black communities and the Atlantic World.[1] As a result, more attention has been given to the ways that Black women and men shaped and were shaped by their connections to the sea. This new scholarship has focused on a wide range of activities by particular individuals, such as Paul Cuffe and James Forten, as well as the influence of certain groups within the African American community, most notably Black seamen.[2] Perhaps the most important contribution of this emerging literature has been how it underscores the multiple ways that maritime life can be linked to competing ideas about race. Our paper is a collaborative effort seeking to highlight the intersection of race, maritime life, and African American history. Specifically, we examine the effort by Marcus Garvey and the Universal Negro Improvement Association (UNIA) to operate a Black-owned steamship line. We argue in part that the success and failure of the Black Star Line is best understood when examined within the broader social, political, economic, and cultural contexts that were mediating the lives of Black people in the post-World War I era. We conclude by offering an assessment of the lasting impact that the Black Star Line had on those most involved in its operation.[3]

MARCUS GARVEY AND THE WORLD HE HELPED MAKE

In 1916, when Marcus Mosiah Garvey arrived in New York City from Kingston, Jamaica, he was already the founder of the fledgling Universal Negro Improvement Association. On the eve of World War I, he had come to the United States ostensibly to embark on a national speaking tour to promote the aims of his recently formed organization. Garvey's hope and expectation at that time was that his American tour would help establish ties within the African American community that could help sustain the UNIA.[4] After a slow and disappointing start, Garvey did establish himself as arguably the most influential voice for the concerns of the African American working class. His message of racial solidarity and economic empowerment through entrepreneurship quickly found a wide audience in Black communities on the verge of the transformations that would accompany the Great Migration.[5] Within the decade, Marcus Garvey and the UNIA grew into the largest African American social, political, and cultural organization ever formed before or since, with a membership estimated at one million at the height of its popularity. The UNIA's influence even stretched beyond the United States as it found members and inspired the founding of similar organizations in Black communities in South Africa, Zimbabwe, Nigeria, Liberia, Brazil, Costa Rica, Panama, and Cuba.[6]

Government officials inside and outside of the United States found the rise of Garvey and UNIA troubling. Great Britain, for example, feared that Garveyism might destabilize its colonial empire in Africa and the Caribbean. The kind of concern Garvey and his movement raised can be heard in the comments of a legislator from Southern Rhodesia's (Zimbabwe's) all-White Legislative Assembly:

> We cannot isolate ourselves; this is a color question, and I will quote what one man said, we have all heard him: Marcus Garvey. He said, "the bloodiest of all wars is yet to come, when Europe will match its strengths against Asia, and that will be the Negroes' opportunity to draw the sword for Africa's redemption." That is what Marcus Garvey said. We can say that he is a raving fanatic and that we ignore him. But every big movement of change in the world that has taken place has been the result of the ravings of a fanatic, as they were called, and ignored in their own day; but history has shown what the ravings of a so-called fanatic are capable of. The seed is sewn and it develops.[7]

Clearly the passion that Marcus Garvey aroused and the opposition that he evoked in the United States and abroad suggest that he and the UNIA represented something important in the lives of many people of African descent. This something was most certainly Black nationalism: the idea that Blacks should form their own nation because they could never achieve justice in America. While Garvey was certainly not the first person to articulate the theme of Black nationalism, his mass movement gave African Americans something that they had never before felt and known so clearly: the sense that they were a collective community who had a shared set of real and

imagined values that could be realized.[8] The world that Garvey culti-
vated through the UNIA encouraged African Americans to embrace,
in the words of Adam Fairclough, "a proud past, a heroic present, and
a magnificent future." Garvey insisted that Blacks were Negroes first
and Americans second. In his view, if 400 million people of African
descent came together, they could liberate Africa from the yoke of
colonialism. They could then create a great African empire that
would embrace all the communities of the African diaspora.[9]

In preparation for this new day in Babylon, the UNIA aimed to
play the role of a government-in-waiting equipped with all of the
trappings of a collective national identity. UNIA members saluted a
flag of red, black, and green, symbolizing the blood shed for liberty,
the color of African people, and the land of their African motherland.
They sang a national anthem: "Ethiopia, Thou Land of our Fathers."
They had as their motto "One God! One Aim! One Destiny!" In the
UNIA's African Orthodox Church, worshippers would pray to a
Black Jesus, a Black God, and hear the slogan chanted, "Africa for
the Africans!" Like any nation that aspires to greatness, the UNIA
boasted of a diplomatic corps, a Great African Army, and a merchant
marine of sorts in the steamships and crew of the Black Star Line.[10]

WISHING ON A BLACK STAR?

Marcus Garvey was not the first person to organize a shipping
scheme as part of a vision of Pan-African renewal and redemption.
That honor belonged to Paul Cuffe, who funded and organized a
voyage in the early nineteenth century. Garvey was not even the first
person of African descent in the post World War I era to put forth the
idea of launching a Black-owned steamship line. The inspiration for
a Black-owned line, according to Robert A. Hill, seems to have been
the brainchild of an itinerant East African known as Prince U Kaba
Rega, who arrived in the United States in 1916.[11] A United States
Bureau of Investigation Informant described him in August of 1920
as "nothing more or less than a Negro agitator attempting to stir up
trouble among the Negroes of this country and the South in particular, exhorting them to radical actions on account of the lynching,
and also exhorting them that they have no flag."[12]

While Prince Kaba Rega devoted most of his time in America to
preaching the gospel, he did confide his hope of returning to Africa

in an April 23, 1918, letter to Robert R. Moton, at the Tuskegee Institute. He wrote: "I have plans by which I will be able to raise a great deal of money from my race for shipping facilities providing that the Government of the United States will grant me the privilege of demonstrating the possibilities and opportunities of the resources of Liberia to my people. I believe within a short time, I can raise enough money from people for the *purchase of a steamship* [authors' emphasis] for the usage of this government and to the credit of my race."[13]

It is unclear what became of Prince Kaba Rega's plan, but it is likely that it failed due to a lack of financial support. Still, his letter is a clear indication that entrepreneurial efforts were very much a part of the thinking of many African Americans.[14]

The environment that nurtured Garvey's shipping venture had its roots in the declining fortunes of the United States Merchant Marine and the racial tension of post-World War I America. Though President Woodrow Wilson had articulated the need for a strong American merchant marine as part of his "New Freedom" program, the United States was largely dependent on foreign-flagged ships to carry out overseas trade. In 1916 (the year Garvey sailed for New York), Congress passed legislation creating the United States Shipping Board to oversee the construction, ownership, and operation of an American merchant fleet for five years. In June of 1917, two months after the U.S. entered the war, the Shipping Board began a massive emergency shipbuilding program designed to transport large numbers of troops and cargoes and formidable enough to sustain the losses caused by German U-boats.[15] When completed, the new fleet was the world's largest merchant marine, equaling 22 percent of the world's shipping, five times the nation's prewar tonnage.[16]

After the armistice, however, the Shipping Board was faced with a glut of surplus vessels and redirected its energies to encourage the sale and private ownership of these vessels, a goal articulated in the preface of the 1920 Merchant Marine Act.[17] The 1920s would see a surge in startup companies. Ethnic organizations such as the Irish Green Star Line and the Polish-American Navigation Company were born during this time of perceived new trade opportunities and anticipated government subsidies. These were for the most part "tramp services," carrying cargo where the need arose and avoiding direct competition with established lines and schedules.[18]

Not surprisingly, some African Americans sought to take advantage of the maritime resources such as surplus ships in ways similar to the efforts of other ethnic groups.The African American Tourist Company, for example, offered cruises to West Africa and the possibility of owning land in Liberia. The African Steamship and Sawmill Company was organized in Philadelphia in 1919.[19]

The *Negro World*, Garvey's weekly newspaper, also celebrated Black-owned shipping, announcing in November 1920 that the West Indian Steamship Company's *John Gully* had safely arrived in Kingston, Jamaica, from the United States. Garvey's article emphasized that the firm was Black-owned, printed the names of the owners, and assured readers that they were all "old and experienced shippers and businessmen."[20]

Garvey's effort to build a Black-owned line was a clear effort to sustain a particular vision of Black liberation. As Judith Stein commented on Garvey's efforts, "ships were the preeminent symbols of national power."[21] Thus the possibility of a Black Star Steamship Line was exciting, romantic, and most importantly a visible expression of Black ambition. For Garvey's followers, the Black Star Line was far more than a commercial venture aimed at producing a profit. It was also a symbol of the possibilities of what Black people could do. The Line represented perhaps the most ambitious effort by an African American organization to channel the gospel of Black nationalism into a tangible symbol of "progress and civilization." The *Negro World* asked readers to consider, "Do you realize this is the only Negro Corporation owning, controlling, and operating steamships in the whole world?"[22] Such rhetorical appeals offered African Americans a clear way to affirm their belief in the potential of Black progress. The rhetoric urging support for the Black Star Line sought to appeal to a need by African Americans to mirror white examples of progress. The first advertisement, published in the April 27, 1919, *New York Call*, captured this sentiment:

> The Universal Negro Improvement Association and African
> Communities League, recognizing, according to its President-General,
> Marcus Garvey, that this is a "selfish age," will hold a mass meeting at
> the Palace Casino, 135th Street and Madison Avenue tomorrow night to
> prove the Negro has caught the spirit. According to Garvey, the Negroes
> are anxious to go back to Africa and the West Indies and create empires
> of their own as that of the yellow and white man. To go back, they need

ships. Therefore at this mass meeting the founding of the "Black Star Line" will be attempted. The proposed steamship line will operate between American ports and those of Africa, West Indies, Central, and South America.[23]

The appeal proved very effective. The Black Star Line offered African Americans a tangible stake in the building of their own merchant marine, and promised non-discriminatory service throughout the Caribbean in the hope of ultimately reaping rich financial rewards from trade with Africa.[24] Within just two and a half years (July 1919-February 1922), the UNIA's aggressive appeals helped the Black Star Line sell over 153,000 shares of stock at $5.00 per share. The 35,000 individual investors not only helped Garvey and the UNIA raise a total of $765,000, they also offered firm proof that African Americans believed they could translate their ideas of progress and modernity into action.[25]

One contemporary observer, Kirnon Hodge, summarized the fundamental quality of Garvey's appeal: "It is to be observed that Garvey is gradually succeeding in idealizing the business end of the UNIA." He declared further that "Garvey is spiritualizing a commercial affair."[26] In galvanizing support within the African American community, the aims of Garvey and the UNIA dovetailed with those of working-class Blacks who had either migrated from the South to cities such as Chicago, Detroit, Cleveland, St. Louis, Washington, Pittsburgh, and New York, or emigrated from Jamaica, Barbados, and Trinidad. These migrants often failed to find the promised land they sought. The Black Star Line offered them a chance to support a venture that fit their expectations of success.

The UNIA, like other contemporary Black-nationalist organizations, did not always advocate for an independent state, but worked to create institutions that historically have formed the backbone of modern nations: schools, civic organizations, literary societies, and businesses. Garvey's idea also meshed well with the speculative mood of the time. It was not uncommon for people of modest means to have purchased Liberty Bonds during the war, and accumulated savings. Consequently, African Americans would not have been reluctant to buy stock in the line, believing that profits were all but guaranteed. An agent of the Bureau of Investigation (precursor to the FBI) attended UNIA meeting in New York's Madison Square Garden and reported back in amazement that Garvey's appeal for funds elicited a "shower of five, ten, and even one-hundred dollar bills" that soon filled "a leather bag of large size to the top."[27]

Garvey's speeches and writings in support of the Black Star Line did not just attract potential investors, but also had a broad emotional appeal for aspiring black mariners. In 1919, the same year the Black Star Line was incorporated, race relations in the United States were in turmoil. Thirty-thousand Black combat troops returned from the war only to discover that their service and sacrifice on the battlefield did not mean the end of racism at home. The servicemen increasingly faced the extra-legal violence of lynch mobs that took offense to Black men in uniform who dared to challenge the illogic of Jim Crow. On the waterfront, Black longshoremen were subjected to similar treatment as they were often erroneously viewed as strike-breaking "scab" laborers who had arrived to help shipping companies quell the increasing labor militancy of white workers.[28]

Black American sailors found that opportunities at sea were as restricted as they were before the war. The United States Navy maintained its exclusionary "messmen" status for Blacks, while the American merchant marine relegated Black sailors to the commissary department. Membership in the Masters, Mates and Pilots Union and the Neptune Association was restricted to "any white person of good moral character." Prospective Black ship operators faced similar racial barriers. In October of 1921, for example, Captain Harry Dean (the great-grandson of Paul Cuffe) petitioned the Emergency Fleet Corporation for vessels. The Shipping Board recommended Dean's request be denied on the basis that whites would refuse to buy vessels used in "colored passenger traffic."[29]

Black sailors Walter S. Sailes, C.B. Joseph, and J.B. Dale expressed their frustration in a letter to the United States Shipping Board in January 1922: "We the undersign [sic] hereby desire to learn from you that if it is through your authority we the colored seamen of the various departments of this city is to be downtrodden and disregarded after our services as citizen has been rendered from time to time. For quite a few weeks now there are lots of shipping from this port and there are men of the above name race who have served in their various lines and we are ignored. . . . So please consider our case as God ordained that every living being must live regardless of race or color."[30]

It seemed that everywhere Black mariners turned they faced the color line. The exception to this was the Black Star Line, where Garvey's shrewd use of advertising was a bold departure from what most Black mariners had come to expect. One circular asked: "Colored Men! Would you like to be Ship Masters? Engineers? Wireless Operators? Would you be proud to have a great line of steamships owned and controlled by MEN of your RACE? Do you believe that Men of your Race can do everything that other men have done? DO and BE."[31]

In many ways, the advertisements were an invitation for adventure and a direct appeal to race pride. Many Black mariners decided to answer in the affirmative.

Joshua Cockburn was the Black Star Line's first captain. A native of the Bahamas with 20 years experience in the Elder Dempster Lines, his status as a British subject meant he was exempt from the restrictions endured by Black American sailors. While on a visit to New York City in July 1919 he offered his services to Garvey. He also attended Black Star Line board meetings and offered to obtain a ship "for the African trade." Cockburn claimed to have many contacts in Africa and told Garvey he has been "commissioned to purchase schooners for trading purposes."[32]

Cockburn's appearance made an immediate and strong impression on Garvey's followers. Garvey spoke of recruiting black captains, but skeptics wondered where he would find the crews and ships to compete in routes dominated by the established shipping companies. To UNIA audiences, the sight of Cockburn "resplendent in his gold-braided English Captain's uniform" brought instant credibility to Garvey's plan. "The very presence of a master mariner" imparted a spirit of buoyancy.[33]

This galvanizing sprit was also instilled in Hugh Mulzac. Born in Union Island (Grenadines) he was, like Cockburn, an experienced mariner. After becoming an American citizen in 1918, he served as a deck officer on both British and American vessels during World War I. Mulzac was the first Black seaman in Baltimore to sit successfully for his master's license. But once he held American citizenship, Mulzac discovered the only work available to him aboard ship was in the steward's department. With a family to support, Mulzac was working as a self-employed wallpaper hanger when he encountered an old friend, Billy Rose, who told him of Garvey's search for black sailors. Mulzac recalled in his autobiography: "Billy's excitement began to seize me, as the hope of sailing on the bridge came alive once more. Maybe this was the answer, the only answer. . . to the shipping operations and all the War shipping Board admirals–a whole fleet of ships owned and operated by black men!" After his first meeting with Garvey, Mulzac left with five shares of stock and "a clear vision of being commander of a great fleet."[34]

Another Black seaman who shared Mulzac's enthusiastic expectation was Captain Adrian Richardson. A native of the West Indies, Richardson was adopted by a Cambridge, Massachusetts, sea captain. Raised and educated on board ship, Richardson earned his master's license in 1919. He found steady work with the Crowell and Thurlow Company. By the 1920s, however, Crowell and Thurlow was in receivership, and Richardson was looking for work. While attending a UNIA rally in Boston, he met Garvey and offered his services, stating "being a colored man myself, I thought I would come and assist you." Richardson was so taken up by the excitement of the Black Star Line that he agreed to work for free, to "help my people."[35]

As each captain would learn, unfortunately, the realties of Garvey's fleet did not live up to the dream, for reasons which had little to do with racial barriers. The first vessel purchased for the Black Star Line was the passenger steamship *Yarmouth*, in 1919. Cockburn participated in the negotiations as broker, netting $1,600 for himself in the process. Previously owned by the North American Steamship Company of Canada, the *Yarmouth* was built in 1877 and worked between Nova Scotia and Boston. During the war, she had been in the transatlantic shipping business, and her war service had left her in need of repairs. The *Yarmouth* was introduced to Black Star Line stockholders as the *Frederick Douglass*, and was "launched" with great fanfare off 135th Street in New York in November 1919. Like Cockburn in his uniform, the *Yarmouth/Frederick Douglass* was a tangible symbol of what could be achieved.[36]

The first voyage of the *Yarmouth* was a cruise from New York to Colon (Panama Canal Zone). With the exception of the first mate and chief engineer, the entire ship's complement was Black. While on the surface it appeared to be a wonderful publicity opportunity for the Black Star Line, Able Seaman Edward Timmy (a member of UNIA) witnessed the inexperience of the crew and their frequent clashes with Cockburn over the issue of wages. It would not be an auspicious beginning for Garvey's fleet.[37]

The *Yarmouth*'s second voyage illustrates how the complexities of running a successful shipping operation would overshadow her value as a propaganda tool. The *Yarmouth* set out on January 16, 1920, to deliver a cargo of Green River Whisky to Cuba, on the eve of Prohibition. The cargo had a value of over one million dollars, but had to be loaded before midnight or confiscated. Cockburn, upset at how UNIA's contract undervalued the cargo, refused to load the ship until its owners compensated by offering him $2,000.00. Since time was running out, the *Yarmouth* was loaded in haste, and once underway began to list. Part of the cargo had to be jettisoned, and the U.S. Coast Guard cutter *Seneca* towed *Yarmouth* back into port on January 19, 1920, two days after the National Prohibition Act became law. If the cargo had been successfully delivered, it would have brought great profits to UNIA and helped prove the viability of a Black-owned steamship line. But similar voyages would end in disaster. Captain Cockburn would later resign and eventually become a successful shipping agent.[38]

Hugh Mulzac was the Chief Officer on the *Yarmouth*'s third voyage, arriving in Havana on March 3, 1920. Mulzac was distressed at the vessel's poor condition (still showing the effects of her whisky cargo mishap), as well as the UNIA's lack of business acumen in failing to arrange for consignees of the cargo. Nevertheless, the crew was greeted in Cuba, Jamaica, and Colon by enthusiastic crowds, including local shippers who proposed switching their carriers to the Black Star Line. Mulzac was "amazed that the *Yarmouth* had become such a symbol for colored people of every land." Ordered by Garvey to make numerous public appearances, the *Yarmouth* finally returned to New York with a cargo of 700 tons of coconuts rotting in the holds.[39]

After a second, equally unsuccessful voyage with the Black Star Line, Mulzac drew up a detailed plan for contracts, loading, and consignments, but the UNIA office never implemented any of his recommendations. Mulzac still maintained hope for the company, describing himself as remaining "an ardent supporter of Garvey, and believe in him, but I never believed in the business methods of the Black Star Line . . . (and) hope that Garvey would eventually turn the operation over to experienced men."[40]

Soon after, Mulzac left the Black Star Line, though he remained optimistic for the future of Black merchant sailors. Back in Harlem, he opened Mulzac's Nautical Academy, teaching young Black men the basics of navigation and preparing them to sit for their licenses. His 52 students were mostly "eager youngsters aflame with the spirit of the Garvey movement."[41]

Meanwhile, Adrian Richardson had been hired as master of the *Kanawa* ("renamed" *Antonio Maceo*). A steam yacht built in 1899 for oil magnate Henry H. Rogers, *Kanawa* was plagued with boiler problems, requiring several expensive repairs. Once again, routine vessel maintenance and operation conflicted with Garvey's use of the ship as a floating ambassador for the UNIA. Though Richardson managed to have *Kanawa* complete a trip from New York to Cuba, his frequent clashes with Garvey came to a head in the summer of 1921. Garvey, wishing to travel but fearing deportation upon his return to New York, signed himself aboard *Kanawa* as chief purser. Richardson left the ship once it reached Jamaica, accusing Garvey of mismanagement and failure to pay the crew.[42]

The Black Star Line's operations were suspended in the spring of 1922, shortly after Garvey's indictment on mail fraud charges in connection with the sale of Black Star Line stock. As the news spread, enrollment in Mulzac's Nautical Academy dropped sharply, with only five of the fifty-two students continuing to attend class. Mulzac recalled the despair articulated by one student: "We can't afford to waste time learning to be officers when there's no future in it for us. The Black Star Line has failed. Even if we get our Third Mate's ticket, where will we get jobs? No white company will hire us."[43]

Mulzac did persuade a few students to remain, including Clifton Lastic and Adolphus Folks. Both went on to earn their licenses and would cross paths with Captain Mulzac several decades later.

Garvey himself took an almost philosophical approach to the Line's fate, writing in the *Negro World*, "Marcus Garvey is not a navigator, he is not a marine engineer, he is not even a good sailor, therefore any individual who would criticize Marcus Garvey for a ship of the Black Star Line not making a success at sea is a fool."[44] Garvey later reflected: "The idea of the Black Star Line has not failed . . . there shall be a greater Black Star Line that shall belt the world with the industries of Black men."[45]

For the mariners, Garvey's dream of Black men at the helm did not die, but was finally realized during the Second World War. Again, the nation's response to wartime shipping needs was to construct an emergency fleet. Liberty Ships (and later Victory Ships) were 7,500 gross-ton, standardized cargo vessels designed to transport troops and materiel to both fronts. The U.S. Maritime Commission named the Liberties after famous Americans, including 17 for "Negroes prominent in national history."[46] Community groups lobbied for specific names. Peter Ross, a Black maintenance foreman at the California Shipbuilding Corporation in the Port of Los Angeles successfully petitioned to name hull 648 in honor of Booker T. Washington.[47] The *Washington* was launched on September 29, 1942, sailing with an integrated crew, and her master was the former Garveyite, Hugh Mulzac. The day he set sail, Mulzac realized he was finally "master of my own vessel. Everything I ever was, stood for, fought for, dreamed of, came into focus that day. . . Being prevented for those twenty-four years from doing the work for which I was trained had robbed life of its most essential meaning."[48]

What must have been equally satisfying to Mulzac was having as Chief Mate Adolphus Folks, a 1922 graduate of Mulzac's own Nautical Academy.[49] Folks's classmate Clifton Lastic sailed as second mate, and Engineer John Garrett also had prior experience aboard Black Star Line ships. A few years later, Lastic would take command of the Liberty Ship *Bert Williams*, named for the famous Black vaudevillian performer. And when the *Frederick Douglass* was launched in Baltimore in 1943, her master was another Black Star Line veteran, Adrian Richardson.[50] Like Mulzac and Lastic, he commanded an integrated crew.[51]

CONCLUSION

Although the Black Star Line is certainly not a case study of successful Black entrepreneurship, it is more than the sum of its parts. The prevailing maritime laws and policies of the 1920s were stacked against startup steamship lines regardless of racial issues, while Garvey's inability to move beyond the venture as anything other than a symbol of racial pride ultimately ensured its demise. Yet the potent symbol of possibility resonated within the individual mariners, who decades later, briefly realized their dreams.[52] Marcus Garvey's Black Star Steamship Line remains as a vivid personification of the dynamic and lasting linkages among seafaring life, race, and maritime history.

Carleton Mitchell photographing Castries Harbor, St. Lucia, 1947.
(© Mystic Seaport, Carleton Mitchell Collection 1996.31.1189)

Carleton Mitchell
and the
Rhetoric *of* Seagoing Dreams

Rosalee Stilwell

It's probably safe to say that few listeners heard Jimmy Buffett singing about "Havana Daydreaming" or "Margaritaville" without dreaming themselves, however briefly, of a life spent sailing through the azure waters of a distant tropical sea. But before there was Jimmy Buffett who wrote about the Great American Escape, there was Carleton Mitchell, the writer who introduced us to that dream before Buffett was even born, and to whom Parrotheads everywhere owe much.

In Carleton Mitchell's first *National Geographic* magazine article, "*Carib* Cruises the West Indies," published in January 1948, he begins with these words: "It is pleasant to have a dream come true, with reality more pleasant than the dream." The yachting cruise he goes on to describe in that essay really was a dream come true for Mitchell, and, in turn, it sparked the dreams of millions of other people who read his words then and who are still reading them now. Even today, anyone who is familiar with Mitchell's life and work knows this man's reality appears to have been what most of us only dream about: a lifetime of sea-going achievement and adventure. Although Carleton Mitchell is justly famous for his seamanship, including three unprecedented and to-date unequaled consecutive wins in the Newport-to-Bermuda sailboat race in the 1950s, his work with the word and image should be regarded as having as much or more impact on the American imagination than his racing accomplishments. Initially Mitchell's work helped to reconfigure the way Americans thought about Caribbean people and places in the latter half of the twentieth century far more than any other writer of our time.

Though it is only possible to examine Mitchell's legacy briefly here, this paper asserts that Mitchell's influence on the worldwide yachting community and Caribbean tourism is largely and powerfully rhetorical. By "powerfully rhetorical" it is meant that Mitchell's work has a persuasive strategy that invites participation by audiences, bringing about a kind of passion for its themes in the hearts and minds of his readers—just the sort of thing good stories have always done.[1] I'm prepared to say, in fact, that Mitchell's writing and photographs created a kind of epideictic rhetoric of sea-going dreams that embodied his rhetorical vision of the Caribbean he loved and that shaped the dreams of a generation. Ultimately, it changed the Caribbean and our understanding of it forever.

To clarify what is meant by such a "rhetorical vision" we can rely on Omar Swartz's definition: "[r]hetorical visions are large meta-narratives (or reality-defining discourses), encapsulated ideologies, [and] prophetic inquiries that suggest alternative possibilities for growth and change. They are symbolically situated desires that have the power to transform images of self, society, and others." Such rhetorical visions have the potential to spread, especially, Ernest Bormann has said, in the hands of those "dream merchants of the mass media" who publish magazines and best-selling books. Mitchell's rhetorical vision did spread, especially at the hands of those "dream merchants" at the National Geographic Society, one of the most powerful entities in the publishing world. The epideictic rhetoric created through the editorial magic of the *National Geographic* differs in interesting ways, though, from the rhetoric Mitchell created in his book, as we shall see.[2]

To continue defining terminology used in this essay, it should be said that "epideictic" is defined as the kind of rhetoric that praises or blames, as epideictic has been traditionally understood. Until recently, though, epideictic rhetoric was thought to be the kind of rhetoric you would hear in windy political speeches, the kind of discourse we might call "hollow bombast" decorated with "gaudy verbal baubles," to quote Celeste Condit. In other words, epideictic was seen as a form of shallow display on the rhetor's part, and, as such, was not considered worthy of much study. In recent years, though, scholars of rhetoric have made it clear that epideictic's appeal is more subtle and more complex than we previously imagined. Rather than being mere display, we now acknowledge that the point of most epideictic rhetoric is to allow the subject's praise or blameworthy qualities to "shine forth" so that audiences gradually apprehend the character of the thing that is being praised or blamed. In this way, epideictic shares many qualities of the dream, and, in fact, much epideictic rhetoric is inspirational and visionary, as in Martin Luther King Jr.'s most famous civil rights speech, in 1964, in which he used the dream as a vehicle. As Dale Sullivan sums it up, epideictic rhetoric doesn't argue, it *invests*. Its appeal can be so subtle, as a matter of fact, that the ancient Greeks felt audiences exposed to such rhetoric were often cleverly seduced into agreement, and thus they believed it to be a very powerful form of persuasion.[3]

The focus for this essay, then, will be only on Carleton Mitchell's epideictic rhetoric in his very first *National Geographic* essay and his first book, *Islands To Windward*, both of which describe a cruise he completed through the Caribbean in the winter of 1947. These two very different publications on the same subject offer scholars a multifaceted look into the ways that people and places of that region were represented to the world during the twentieth century, documenting an era of Caribbean life that is gone forever. As well, they offer us a look into the ways that one event can be envisioned in two different and very powerful ways. If one vision is disseminated to a wider audience through the expertise of those "dream merchants," it isn't hard to understand, then, why it becomes the more believed dream by more people in the end.

In order to accept this thesis, though, it's important to understand Carleton Mitchell's considerable success as a writer and a photographer and thus how far his influence reached at the height of his publishing career. Of the seven books he published between the years 1948 and 1971, three went into second editions and one was translated into French and Spanish. *Islands To Windward*, published in 1949, was, during the 1950s and 60s, often referred to as "the Bible of Caribbean cruising" because of its impact on the sailing community. Mitchell also published 11 articles in *National Geographic* (as pointed out before, one of the most popular magazines on the planet), the majority of which were about the Caribbean region, not to mention innumerable essays for *Yachting* and *Sports Illustrated*. His photographic output equals if not exceeds his body of writings: The Carleton Mitchell Collection at Mystic Seaport numbers over 20,000 images, representing at least six decades of maritime photography, with a large percentage of the collection focused on Caribbean people and places. Truly, Mitchell is a man who has given scholars a lot to explore in terms of his textual and visual expressions of race, ethnicity, and power in the Americas.[4]

But how influential was Carleton Mitchell's work, you might wonder? When beginning this inquiry, the writer was curious if the popularity of Mitchell's work (and especially *Islands To Windward* and his essays for *National Geographic*) could be correlated to any actual growth in recreational yachting and tourist industries in the Caribbean. An investigation into statistics on the growth of yachting and general tourism in the Caribbean was undertaken in an effort to clarify this question. Although I realize claiming that Carleton Mitchell is entirely responsible for the billion-dollar boom in travel to the Caribbean would be irresponsible, I was nevertheless struck by the strong parallel between Mitchell's publishing career on the topic and the rise in yachting and general tourism in the Caribbean region. Not surprisingly, economic growth charts on the subject of Caribbean tourism, for instance, show that American tourism accelerated rapidly in the 1950s and 1960s, those years in which Mitchell was actively publishing on the topic. The growth in yachting and land-based tourism through the Caribbean was, of course, phenomenal in those years, as it has continued to be in recent years. As well, *National Geographic* experienced its sharpest rise in circulation rates between 1948 (the year Mitchell's first article appeared) and 1972, when his last essay was included, from 1.5 million subscribers to over 10 million. Sole credit cannot be given to him for the growth in Caribbean yachting *and* the enormous circulation of *National Geographic*, but these numbers show that Mitchell was writing something that sold, and sold big. It was a rhetoric of sea-going epideictic dreams that held immense attraction for a great many people.[5]

One of the curious aspects of his early writing on the Caribbean in *Islands To Windward* (his first book) and his first *National Geographic* article is that they are, as "rhetorical visions" or "reality-defining discourses," quite different. The people of the Caribbean, for instance, are presented in different ways in the article and in the book. Much of this difference has to do with writing style. As Mitchell says in the oral history he recorded for Mystic Seaport in 1997, *National Geographic* editors instructed writers to use the first-person pronoun in short, declarative sentences with plenty of exclamation marks to signal even the simplest humor to the reader. This particular "easy to interpret" style is distinctive of the *National Geographic*, as other researchers have shown. Catherine Lutz and Jane Collins, for example, detail how the Society's "seven principles" of publication, which were guidelines conceived in 1915 and followed until very recently, determined the content and style of articles that appeared in the magazine. The "seven principles" state, in part, that the Society would only publish entirely accurate information and "only what is of a kindly nature . . . [with] everything unpleasant or unduly critical being avoided." In regard to the magazine's photographs, the Society wished them to be "beautiful (aesthetically pleasing), artistic (or embodying certain conventions of high-brow art), and instructive (realistic in representation)." As Lutz and Collins explained in their book, *Reading National Geographic*, "[w]hat [*National Geographic*] writers accomplished by an insistently upbeat and uncomplicated style [accompanied by] the erasure of conflicting points of view, and the presentation of names, dates, and numbers was reinforced by the codes of photographic realism." So there you have it: the magazine packaged a distinct, easy-to-understand, and well-intentioned picture of the world for its reading public, a vision of the world that is pleasant and pretty and quite uncomplicated. If you compare Mitchell's *National Geographic* article to his book, the difference between the two, this deliberate shaping of rhetorical vision, is striking.[6]

First, Mitchell's *National Geographic* article is faithful to the Society's principles by not including any of the unpleasant, troubling, or difficult aspects of Caribbean life in the 1940s. Every day is a sunny day in *National Geographic*'s Caribbean. All the people are happy, and the average person is pretty good looking, to paraphrase Garrison Keillor. The book, *Islands To Windward*, on the other hand, provides readers with the troubling and even gruesome details regarding the extermination of native peoples, of the Africans brought there in slavery, of the poverty and isolation of island life as Mitchell perceived them in 1947. Second, in the magazine article, the captions were written by editors, not the author, and the proper names of Caribbean people of color are not likely to be mentioned. In the book, Mitchell wrote his own captions, and it is clear that people of color get named more often and pictured more often.[7] In his book, Mitchell's captions directly relate to the photographs, but in the magazine article, as happened in many *National Geographic* articles of this period, captions may not relate to photographs at all, for reasons discussed below. Third, the magazine text dwells much longer on what we might call the "white history" of the region–those events and personalities that highlight European accomplishments and activities. You might imagine, in fact, from the text of the magazine article, that a cruise through the Caribbean was indeed a long, fair-weather cruise through a paradise untroubled by its bloody history–most of which was authored

by Europeans. In his book, however, Mitchell spends much more time incorporating the social history of various Caribbean peoples into his narrative, documenting their struggle against oppression with a great deal of sympathy. He also includes passages about bad weather and discomforts and all sorts of challenges in general that *National Geographic* excluded–an interesting difference that it seems would whet the appetites of sailors much more than the more sanguine world depicted in the magazine article.

At this point, it should be acknowledged that Mitchell's presentation in either publication would not satisfy the current appetite for cultural deconstruction, but even so, the *National Geographic* Caribbean impresses one as a sanitized paradise waiting to be discovered, in marked contrast to the version of it we read in Mitchell's book. It's not hard to see, even from this brief listing of differences between the magazine article and the book, that the vision of a Caribbean cruise could be perceived quite differently by the much larger audience of the magazine than by the relatively small audience of the book. It attests to Mitchell's skill as a writer that his *National Geographic* article is so well written that its more reductive view of the Caribbean people and places is still enjoyable and informative to read. One has to wonder, though, what differences in readers' perceptions of the region resulted from each text.

In the course of the research for this project, the author's communications with Mitchell on the subject of writing both pieces shed some light on those choices all professional writers must face. These exchanges have considerably altered this author's understanding of the rhetorical situation Mitchell faced and, consequently, broadened an appreciation for the choices that all writers in similar situations must face. Mitchell felt, for example, that he should be able to simplify his style because he considered such flexibility of style to be a mark of professionalism. More importantly, he indicated that he was well aware of a different side to island life, but it was a perspective that he deliberately did not include. Mitchell recorded that had he included this troubled side of Caribbean life there was a good chance that his work might not have found a publisher at the time. It should be added that, Mitchell's finely tuned sense of good manners and fair play also precluded writing about anything that could be construed as an attack on people who most probably would not have had the means to rebut his commentary. Speaking to this point, he explicitly stated that he didn't go out seeking adventure deliberately so that he could sell adventure stories. Instead, he went to see how other everyday people were living their everyday lives. In this way, he ended up creating an epideictic rhetoric that praised the people who became "real" to him, with whom he spent a good number of years, and whom he thought of as friends, not as subjects of ethnographic research or social activism. The complexity of Mitchell's rhetorical choices in his representation of Caribbean people should give us pause as we consider what we ourselves might do in a similar situation.[8]

Given that his writing and his photography do center around the everyday life of Caribbean people he got to know, and who got to know him, he would consider it unforgivably rude to display for an audience of millions some unfortunate situation in the life of some real person to whom he felt a social obligation, as anyone might feel toward an acquaintance. In fact, we can dare to extrapolate from the comments he has made that he felt himself to be strongly connected to those people he met in the Caribbean during that cruise and in the decades he has lived and traveled there since. When considering his work from his authorial perspective, the responsibility of authors to those people of different cultures they write about becomes clear. Mitchell, after all, involves himself in the lives of real people with feelings who might read what he had written about them.

Viewed in this way, his representation of his subjects takes on a different motive than that which we in academe almost always these days attribute to European-Americans abroad in previous decades.

In the current critical climate, readers are very quick to attribute exploitive motives to an elite Southern white man in a yacht wandering around tropical islands. Many expect him to be seeking out the exoticized version of island life in order to examine it under the mass-mediated lens of American superiority for his own fame and profit. Is this assumption fair? Or is it a new stereotype? Though we often correctly criticize such exploitation by members of our society past and present, in Mitchell's case we still have the luxury of asking what his rhetorical restraints actually were—and we find out he had complex ethical concerns that shaped his representation of what he saw. He had to make those choices necessary for his own writing career while, at the same time, balancing what he perceived to be his duty toward his friends at the time. He praised what he saw as valuable to praise, and let the rest go. Through the contemplation of Mitchell's rhetorical and ethical constraints we must reconsider the work of writers who drop into the lives of others, pose as sympathetic friends, then return home to publish their version of the truth about some other culture's way of life as they see it. Mitchell's work might help us reevaluate not only older accounts of other cultures but a number of those contemporary "intra-cultural" accounts of our own society by writers such as Mike Rose, Jonathan Kozol, and Herbert Kohl, all of whom have written eloquently but excoriatingly of American students and teachers, for instance. How do these writers interpret and act upon the ethical obligation to those whom they write about? What are the responsibilities and restraints incumbent upon these observers? Have they exploited the confidence of those they observed, though their intentions are seemingly above reproach? Mitchell's experience can deepen our appreciation for the nuances of representation in ways that this writer has only just begun to understand.

One way to explore Mitchell's epideictic vision of the Caribbean is to study the photographs that *National Geographic* editors used for his article and compare them with those images used in his book and those images that he considered his favorites and subsequently put into albums, which are now held by Mystic Seaport. Such a three-way comparison offers insight on the type of visual imagery the National Geographic Society valued, the type of visual imagery Mitchell himself thought proper to publish, and the visual imagery he personally enjoyed.

Reviewing those images in the *National Geographic* is especially interesting when we realize that the Society's own marketing researchers have found 53 percent of the magazine's subscribers will *only* view an article's photographs and *might* read the captions, as opposed to reading the whole essay. Scholars who have studied the rhetorical vision of race, class, and ethnicity in the Society's publications have noticed certain consistent features of the magazine's photographs, especially those issues published between 1896 (when the first photographs appeared) and 1980 (when many editorial changes occurred at the magazine). Some of those characteristics are discussed below, but it should be pointed out first that these consistent tendencies show that *National Geographic* does carefully shape its own rhetorical vision so that readers are not threatened, disturbed, or otherwise confronted by aspects of race, class, and ethnicity.[9]

Mitchell illustrated the magazine essay with photographs that he took on the cruise. Those photographs, though, were chosen and then captioned by editors, not Mitchell himself. The images that found their way into the article (all of them "pleasant" and "pretty" and undisturbing in ways that I will discuss) are different from the photographs that Mitchell selected as his own favorites in the two albums I mentioned. His book, on the other hand, has a mixture of both.[10]

One sort of image that is consistently found throughout all three sources is that of the sublimely beautiful tropical landscape. At first glance, the magazine article, his book, and his albums are saturated with beautiful landscapes. Visions of paradise are, of course, a staple of *National Geographic*, as they are of almost every book on the Caribbean. But of all American magazines, *National Geographic* in particular is known for its landscapes and its happy people who don't look too old, too poor, or too angry, and who live in a perpetually sunny world. This is how the Society stayed true to its principles to be fair, uncritical, and controversial in its coverage of the world. It praised, in its subtle epideictic fashion, what it wanted to praise about the world and its peoples.

This vision of a "middle class world," as Lutz and Collins have called it, is a consistent feature of *National Geographic* on the whole and has to do with the magazine's vision of cultural difference: it is most often portrayed in ways that our society finds "beautiful" and not disturbing.[11] As mentioned above, that means that the ugly, the poor, and the old don't often get portrayed in the magazine's pictures. As well, people of color are portrayed in idealized ways as happy, close to the sacred, close to nature, with a strong work ethic, and as "gentle"–that is, not given to violence. Men are also often shown as acting out important cultural roles such as in war or religious rituals or doing the important work of the community. It praised those things about other cultures in such a way that would be nonthreatening and "safe" to the readership back home.

It's also interesting to note that Lutz and Collins found that the magazine consistently pictured very dark-skinned people 28 percent

Woman with Laura,
"the man-hating
parrot of
Basseterre,"
St. Kitts, 1947.
(© Mystic Seaport,
Carleton Mitchell
Collection
1996.31.1390)

Crew of the
coconut sloop
Concordia, 1947.
(© Mystic Seaport,
Carleton Mitchell
Collection
1996.31.5998.26)

of the time over the years, while 12 percent of the people shown were "white" or light colored, but fully 60 percent of the people pictured were considered by researchers to be "bronze" colored. Bronze, not black, was arguably the most interesting color you could be to American audiences–especially if you were a woman. Men were pictured nearly two-thirds of the time in the magazine, with women appearing about half as often. In Mitchell's article and in his book, my own count shows that dark people appear about as regularly as bronze or white people do.[12]

National Geographic's positioning and costuming of women in its photographs is also very interesting. Women are often shown posed against a "halo of green," calling forth visions of delicate and endangered birds whose colorful plumage surprises and delights the eye. In fact, women pictured in the *National Geographic* are frequently very young and beautiful and bronze-colored. Researchers find that the "halo" images are nearly *always* inhabited by that type. Women are also often posed in passive or self-reflexive ways that Irving Goffman says characterizes women's supposed self-involvement. As well, they are often posed in clean, new indigenous costume, or in some other way that exposes a good deal of bare skin. In general, we might say that women were much more likely to be eroticized in the magazine: as every schoolboy knows, the *National Geographic* was famous for its "bare-breasted brown ladies" (and that's Carleton Mitchell's own joking description of the phenomenon, by the way) with a caption addressing, as Mitchell pointed out, last year's copra production (or something equally as unrelated to the photograph).[13]

Mitchell's photographs in both his book and his *National Geographic* article do not conform to the standard Society vision of feminine beauty as a bare-skinned 16-year-old posed like an exotic bird in front of green foliage. Instead, his photographs are of women of diverse ethnicities, races, ages, and classes as they went about their jobs and lived their lives in the Caribbean of the 1940s. What the magazine printed, however, were the shots he took of blonde tourists and young women, not the old matriarchs who actually conducted business with him or even the poor, threadbare, working-class women who figured in much of his photography. This is not to say, however, the editors of *National Geographic* failed to get a bare-breasted lady in Mitchell's first article for them. They did.

It's a statue made from the ashes of St. Pierre, Martinique, after the explosion of Mt. Pelee in 1902 and portrays a suitably bare-breasted female figure arising out of the ashes.

In *National Geographic*, it was also much more common for men of color to be shown as looking away from the camera rather than directly into it, especially if they were in groups. And everybody was usually shown smiling. As some of the photographers for *National Geographic* have recently revealed, it was felt by editors that a direct, assertive, and unsmiling gaze by black people in a group could be disturbing to the magazine's audience. A fascinating example of how Society editors could shape the portrayal of black men in its pages is that of the "Hellcats," a steel drum band that Mitchell photographed on Grenada. He took many different shots of the band and their audience, from different angles and in different lighting. The photograph of the Hellcats that made its appearance in the magazine shows a group of men all anomically looking away from the camera—something that Lutz and Collins find to be usual in the representation of black men in groups. In Mitchell's book, the band members look entranced, listening closely to their own sound as any orchestra would during tune-up time. In his personal album, they can be seen to be swigging from bottles, and, it looks like to this observer, smoking homemade cigarette-like objects. They look directly into the camera—some with very pleasant expressions and some with vacant stares. It makes an interesting study to consider the progression of the Hellcats from magazine to book to album. It's also interesting that Mitchell took many pictures of children in the audience—junior Hellcats, perhaps?—that didn't make it into either forum. These children, mostly boys, aren't smiling. They are, perhaps, even returning the gaze of the camera a little confrontationally. As mentioned earlier, these images were not printed in either Mitchell's article or his book.[14]

It is hoped that this brief presentation of Mitchell's two texts has demonstrated that his personal epideictic rhetoric was one that was more textured, more rounded, and more progressive than perhaps the one developed for him by the National Geographic Society editors. His writing was powerful and interesting enough to create a groundswell of interest in the Caribbean that changed that region of the world forever. Even today, it's possible to read Mitchell's books, fall in love with his vision of the Caribbean, and dream your own seagoing dreams without ever having a Jimmy Buffett lyric cross your mind. For serious scholarly study in the future, Mitchell's work should be closely examined for its contribution not only to our cultural rhetoric about the Caribbean and its people, but also for the presence of its American maritime and literary themes. His books offer a wealth of rhetorical devices to study, from, for instance, their complex embedded narratives to their overarching rhetorical vision. As well, his photographs more than merely augment his textual work. They are a veritable treasure-trove of visual representation of race, ethnicity, and class just waiting to be explored and commented upon by scholars of visual rhetoric. Taken together, they represent American epideictic dreaming in real time, one that is not only worthwhile to study, but also one that still remains a pleasure to read and enjoy.

The Mississippi Gulf Coast:

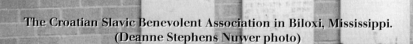

The Croatian Slavic Benevolent Association in Biloxi, Mississippi.
(Deanne Stephens Nuwer photo)

Casting a *Wide* Cultural Net

Deanne Stephens Nuwer

On the Gulf of Mexico's northern rim between Mobile, Alabama, and New Orleans, Louisiana, is a cultural enclave distinct from the rest of the American South. That region is the Mississippi Gulf Coast. Biloxi, Mississippi, one town along this Coast, exemplifies the cultural gumbo of the area and is a prime model of the various cultures found in this third coastal region.

Biloxi is a city of great ethnic and cultural diversity, with a French Catholic base not found elsewhere in Mississippi. In 1699, Pierre LeMoyne, Sieur d'Iberville, founded Biloxi Bay Colony while under the commission of King Louis XIV of France. Biloxi was the first permanent settlement in Lower French Louisiana and served as its capital from 1719 to 1722. In fact, it was the prototype for the later capital, New Orleans, Louisiana.[1]

The French ruled the Louisiana Territory, including Mississippi, for 64 years and left behind a rich cultural heritage. After the French and Indian War, England assumed control of the Mississippi region in 1763, and Spain governed the area until 1798, when Mississippi officially became a United States territory. After territorial status, Mississippi became the twentieth state in the Union on December 10, 1817. By that time, its Gulf Coast was a great cultural melting pot with Spanish, French, Native American, Caribbean, African, British, Irish, and Scottish inhabitants all contributing to the coastal settlement's personality.

Nestled between New Orleans and Mobile, the Coast continued to attract diverse ethnic groups who developed and improved the region. By 1838, when Biloxi was incorporated as a town, it was recognized as a resort area with hotels, boardinghouses, and summer cottages attracting visitors. In 1847, the Biloxi lighthouse was erected to guide ships to a safe harbor. The population was approximately 600 during this time.[2]

Shortly after the Civil War, construction of the New Orleans, Mobile & Chattanooga Railroad began. This railroad line spanned the entire Gulf Coast area by 1870.[3] Railroad passenger service allowed more winter visitors and settlers to flock to the Mississippi Gulf Coast, where they were attracted by the mild winters and by the burgeoning timber industry along the myriad bayous and backwater coastal areas.

Included in the settlers' numbers were emigrants from the Dalmatian Coast on the Adriatic Sea, who were seeking sanctuary from the turbulent political system in their homeland. The immigrants soon incorporated themselves into the oyster industry that was slowly developing in the Biloxi area. They ultimately contributed a new type of boat construction called the lugger to the oyster industry. Initially, oystermen tonged from white-winged Biloxi schooners, but by the 1920s the Slavonian-inspired lugger had almost completely replaced the sleek schooners. The lugger was "a low, sturdy, wide-beamed fishing boat ideally suited to the shoal waters of the [Mississippi] sound." Men could work safely from it, and a smaller crew than a schooner's could harvest shrimp and oysters from this gasoline-powered boat.[4]

Although shrimp were very plentiful in the Gulf waters, the shrimp industry lagged behind the oyster industry in its initial development. One explanation was that shrimp have a natural acid that, when canned, caused them to turn black. The acid also created iron and tin sulfide deposits in tin cans during early efforts at marketing the crustaceans.[5] In order for seafood entrepreneurs to be successful with shrimp and establish a thriving enterprise, the industry needed an improved technology.

George W. Dunbar, originally from a Bridgewater, Massachusetts, shoe-manufacturing family, began experimenting with shrimp when he first arrived in New Orleans, Louisiana. By 1867 the Dunbar family found success by emulating French canning methods for shrimp. To stop the discoloration, Dunbar lined the tin shrimp cans with muslin bags. However, in 1875, artificial ice manufacturing improved, and with that technology fresh seafood could be shipped inland as far as Memphis, Tennessee. Simultaneously, a new process of canning shrimp with parchment liners expanded the commercial potential for this seafood.[6]

With the introduction of dry ice and these improved canning methods, Lazaro Lopez, F. William Elmer, W.K. Dukate, William Gorenflo, and James Maycock put together $8,000 of combined capital and formed the Lopez, Elmer, and Company seafood packing endeavor. This was the first packing enterprise in Biloxi. The facility opened on Biloxi Back Bay at the foot of Renoir Street in 1881. The company canned oysters and shrimp and offered raw oysters in bulk during season. When not processing seafood, the company also canned figs.[7]

By 1882, other investors located the Barataria Canning Company in the Point Cadet area of Biloxi, seeking profits from the expanding shrimp and oyster industry. Five canneries existed by 1885. As a result of increased seafood production, companies required larger labor pools than Biloxi offered. The solution to this problem was discovered by one of the initial investors, W.K. Dukate. Dukate traveled to the oyster port of Baltimore, Maryland, to learn the latest seafood-canning procedures and to acquaint himself with the new equipment and labor management techniques that growth demanded. While there, he realized that Biloxi's labor needs could be met by the "Bohemian" or Polish seasonal workers he found laboring in Baltimore's canneries.[8]

Because of the expanding seafood industry, Biloxi's population increased from 1,500 in the 1880s to 3,234 by 1890. Obviously, the Gulf Coast town was thriving because of its maritime connection. The shrimp/oyster industry was flourishing, and orders poured in at an astounding rate. On January 11, 1890, the Sea Coast Packing Company imported the first transient workers whom Dukate had observed while in Baltimore. The local townspeople, curious about the newcomers, turned out to observe the immigrants when they arrived in Biloxi by train. The local newspaper reported that "a close examination proved that they had neither tails nor tusks, but were very much like other people." The Sea Coast Packing Company built long row houses or camps that were dubbed the "Hotel d'Bohemia" for the workers. Other seafood factories soon followed Sea Coast's lead, and Baltimore workers flooded into the city. One Biloxian, Amelia "Sis" Eleuteris, recalled that the Polish laborers spoke English and "were good-natured." She also commented that these workers built their own communal brick ovens on the seafood companies' campgrounds and baked their bread in them. The Polish workers also enjoyed music and dancing the polka in the camps. Often, accordion music wafted over the city as the workers gathered after a day's labor. According to Eleuteris, the Polish workers' wages were "pitiful" because their train passage to Biloxi was deducted from their earnings. These workers continued to migrate to Biloxi for 28 years as itinerant laborers, and some chose to remain in the Gulf Coast region where many of their descendants live today. The last of the seafood workers's camps disappeared with Hurricane Camille in 1969 and urban renewal in the 1970s.[9]

As a result of the seafood industry's expansion and Biloxi's population growth, Back Bay and Point Cadet underwent enormous transitions. These two areas in the city had a concentrated workforce and seafood factories in close proximity to one another, thereby creating unprecedented economic opportunities. Moreover, because of the unique working and housing situation in those two areas, cultural identity remained intact as seafood camps acted as insulators from outside influences on the workers' ethnicity.[10]

By 1892, Biloxi's seafood industry eclipsed earlier production predictions. With the advent of the steam oyster dredge for harvesting the bivalves and resulting regulations of the oyster industry, Biloxi, by 1903, acquired the title, "Seafood Capital of the World." Twelve canneries reported a combined harvest of 5,988,788 pounds of oysters and 4,424,000 pounds of shrimp. Biloxi's population had swelled to approximately 8,000.[11]

Shortly thereafter, Biloxi's seafood industry evolved as new labor forces joined the ranks of workers and individual boat ownership became more accessible. Prior to World War I, the seafood factory owners controlled all aspects of the industry, owning the factory that canned the shrimp and oysters as well as the schooners that caught the bounty. Schooners cost approximately $2,200 ready for sea, therefore pricing the average laborer out of individual ownership. As a result of the introduction of gasoline-powered boats after 1914, and the implementation of the otter trawl that required only two men to haul it onto a boat, schooner production fell along with the prices of seafood. In 1906, Biloxi had 327 schooners, but by 1914 only 277 remained. Simultaneously, motor-powered fishing vessels increased from 78 to 106. Local fishermen were able to purchase or finance the less-expensive gasoline-powered luggers individually or in partnerships and begin harvesting shrimp and oysters to sell to those seafood factories that survived the World War I slump. Luggers cost approximately $800 if they were not outfitted with an engine and other equipment, or $1,000 if sea-ready. In time, a new phase of Biloxi's seafood industry began.[12]

Participating in the ownership opportunities of the gasoline-powered luggers were two new immigrant groups, the Slavs and Louisiana Cajuns. The original few Slavs, mostly Croats, with Serbs and Slavonians comprising a smaller percentage, had migrated to Biloxi prior to World War I. They were from Dalmatia, along the

Adriatic Sea, and inland Croatia, Bosnia-Herzagovina, and Serbia. Seeking economic freedom, men from these regions migrated to and extolled the advantages of maritime Mississippi through letters home. Others soon followed, relying upon their countrymen's descriptions of the vast opportunities waiting in maritime Biloxi. As a result, a tide of Slavonian men toiled to earn passage for their families after entering Biloxi's seafood industry. When their families received the long-awaited ticket money from Biloxi, the immigration authorities in New York City identified them by placing a tag on their coat directing the train conductor to route them to Biloxi. One writer commented that as a result of these immigrants, "there was the solid foundation of the Dalmation colony in eastern Biloxi, the hard working backbone of the growing and expanding shrimp and oyster fame of Biloxi."[13]

Once in their new home, the women and children quickly sought employment in the picking sheds at the seafood factories, where they earned "shrimp nickels." Factory workers received about a penny a pound for picking shrimp. When pickers filled a five-pound bucket, they were paid a nickel. The shrimps' acid caused nickels to turn green, so local merchants often had green-tinged cash registers. In an effort to avoid green nickels, the canners eventually minted their own tokens that indicated the amount of shrimp or oysters picked by the employee. Local banks even accepted these tokens as currency until the federal government halted the action, claiming the tokens were a form of counterfeit currency. Today, seafood tokens are collectors' items that conjure images of back-breaking work and bygone days.[14]

Another wave of immigrants, the Acadians from Louisiana, also came to Biloxi during the first half of the twentieth century. The first to arrive did so on July 25, 1914. They were welcomed to their own "CC Camps" or "Canner's Camps" by the factory owners. Sharing two common denominators–Catholicism and familiarity with shrimp and oysters–with the other cultural groups then living on Biloxi's Point Cadet, the Acadians settled into their maritime environment, adding to the growing diversity of the city.[15]

The Acadians were promised steady employment and wood for their stoves if they emigrated to Biloxi to work in the seafood factories. Most who moved were small farmers or sharecroppers who had felt the grip of economic hard times when the sugarcane crops failed in their native state. Louisiana workers came from such places as New Iberia, Lafayette, and Broussard. Removed from its insular rural environment, the Cajun culture diffused and intertwined with the Slavonian traditions, creating a unique culture developed within the Biloxi seafood industry.[16]

One Louisianaian who settled into Biloxi's seafood industry was Ellison Hebert. Born in New Iberia in 1906, he and his family moved to Biloxi when he was 18. Working first for the Fountain Company on a shrimper powered by sail, he eventually owned his own gasoline-powered boat, the *Whipporwill.* According to Hebert, a 210-pound barrel of shrimp fetched $4.00 when brought in for sale. He stated that, as a shrimper, he had a "beautiful life but you'd never be home."[17]

Cajuns and Slavonians entered the various aspects of maritime employment essentially at the same economic level, as fishermen or factory workers. Each group adapted to working in close proximity to the other. They came into daily contact on Biloxi's two-square-mile peninsula of Point Cadet and Back Bay, living and working together. They mingled freely but also maintained cultural differences and customs. Their daily lives were affirmations of ethnic identity as well as continuous intercultural exchanges. Thus, French bread and Slavonian pusheratas, gumbo and fish stew, *fais do-do* dancing and oyster shucking contests, and the Marinoviches and Heberts all mixed to create multi-cultural Biloxi.[18]

However, the occupational identity of Slavic immigrants and Acadian French reinforced their ethnicities through club associations. For example, on December 26, 1912, local Slavonian seafood workers chartered the Austrian Benevolent Association. Jake Stanovich, Nick Skrmetta, and Victor Simonich were its first officers as 50 charter members signed the roll. The Society's purpose was to provide sickness and death benefits for members and their families, which was supported by the $1.00 fee. Families received $200 for a death and $10 per month for sickness for a ten-month maximum in any one year.[19]

After Emperor Franz Joseph's Austrian Empire crumpled, the Austrian Association created a new charter in 1918 and changed its name to the Slovinsko Dobrotverno Drustvo, or the Slavonian Benevolent Association of St. Nicola. Soon, the Ladies Auxiliary became a very active part of the Lodge, and the Slavonians participated in the Annual Blessing of the Fleet and the Schooner races. These races lasted until 1932, when gasoline engines finally replaced sail power.[20] Today, a new building on the corner of Myrtle and First Streets boasts a statue of St. Nicola, the Lodge's patron saint. On either side of the statue are stone tablets engraved with the names of Slavonian families who settled in Biloxi.

In 1932, at Clarence Boudwin's home, 25 Cajun seafood workers and boat captains chartered the Fleur-de-Lis Society in Biloxi. Like the Slavonian Lodge (and other American mariners' associations activities since the eighteenth century) the Fleur-de-Lis Society's original purpose was to help care for sick and poor fishermen and to help offset funeral expenses. Dues were set at $.50 monthly, and the Society promised "a decent burial without worry or burden on the widow." The organization stipulated that members had to have French ancestry proven for three generations and had to speak French.[21] The group eliminated the language requirement in 1952, but French ancestry is still mandatory today. Its 1954 building on Howard Avenue hosts a variety of social functions. The Fleur-de-Lis Society is a driving force behind the annual Biloxi Seafood Festival and Blessing of the Fleet.

Education was an integral part of Point Cadet and Back Bay Biloxi life, with the Dukate, Gorenflo, Howard, and Lopez families contributing land, building materials, and money to the city for the education of Biloxi's citizens, regardless of socioeconomic standing or ethnic origins. In fact, citizens from the Point Cadet area circulated a petition in 1891 for a school for factory workers' and fishermen's children.[22]

By 1894, branch schools were in the Point Cadet region, and by 1896 Biloxians living on the Point had a permanent school. Miss Margaret Speir established the Naturalization School of Point Cadet in 1920. Even though the school existed for only one year, it was vital in teaching basic United States citizenship requirements to Slavonian immigrants. Speir operated the school from 6:00 to 9:00 P.M. so that seafood factory work schedules were not interrupted.[23] Given that the commitment to public education was firmly established among The Point and Back Bay inhabitants, her efforts were well received among the area's populace.

After World War II, the Biloxi seafood industry began another evolutionary cycle. During the Great Depression and war years, a new employer arrived in Biloxi on June 12, 1941: Keesler Air Force Base. The once-great canning factories began to give way to other industries, as second-generation fishing families migrated into new occupations not connected to maritime endeavors. Although the seafood culture remained alive in the Slavonian and Acadian social organizations and in local festivities, shipbuilding became more profitable as did the increasing tourist trade in the 1950s. Gambling and the "high life" were the economic cornerstones of many clubs located further west, away from Point Cadet and Back Bay Biloxi.[24]

Through the 1960s and 1970s, the Point Cadet neighborhoods experienced difficult economic times as seafood sources expanded to include foreign providers and the cost of fishing boats increased. Overfishing also added to the precarious position of some fisher-men and factories. Moreover, Hurricane Camille devastated much of the Mississippi Gulf Coast, including its fishing fleets and man-ufacturers, in 1969. However, as a result of this mass destruction, some fishermen benefited in the aftermath of the killer storm when low-interest government loans became available. Larger boats with new technological devices now created a year-round seafood business, as Biloxi vessels sought shrimp in deeper, more distant waters.[25]

The 1970s also heralded the arrival of a new immigrant group to the Biloxi area. After the fall of South Vietnam in 1975, many Vietnamese arrived in the United States, seeking political asylum. The slumping fisheries lured the Vietnamese into the already multi-ethnic seafood industry in Biloxi. Despite their cultural and language differences, their connection to a maritime economy left behind in Vietnam enticed many of the immigrants to settle in the Point Cadet and Back Bay areas of the city. The Catholic Diocese of Biloxi primarily helped to establish them in the region. Many of the new immigrants had two commonalities with other inhabitants: the Vietnamese refugees were Catholic and fishermen.[26]

The original 1,300 Vietnamese immigrants who arrived in Biloxi were from Vung Tau, once a resort and fishing town in South Vietnam.[27] They migrated to Empire, Louisiana, first and later came eastward to Biloxi. By 1983, 2,000 Vietnamese lived in Biloxi. According to one Vietnamese man, "in Biloxi, people don't seem to mind so much if we come."[28]

At first the Vietnamese secured employment in areas that were not desirable to others. They shucked oysters and picked crabs. St. Michael's Catholic Church, located on Point Cadet near the Old Cannery Row of seafood factories, became the center of life for extended Vietnamese families arriving from their homeland. Most Biloxians' attitudes toward the Vietnamese reflected respect because the new arrivals worked long hours and diligently. One Biloxian, Todd Rosetti, whose family has worked for generations in the seafood industry, stated, "If it wasn't for the Vietnamese fishermen, the industry would have nearly disappeared." The Covacivich family rented space to the immigrants so that they could build their boats. Chuong Phan, owner of the 64-foot shrimper *Fatima Lady II*, remarked in an interview, "Everything that looks like it works not so good, we fix it." Phan left Vietnam in 1979 and (after living elsewhere) arrived in Biloxi in 1986.[29]

Vietnamese shrimpers, because of a language barrier, also had to be educated about shrimping under American cultural mores and U. S. Coast Guard regulations. For example, the Vietnamese shrimpers learned to shrimp east-to-west rather than their traditional north-to-south routine. By doing so, the immigrants would not foul other shrimpers' nets. They also needed to learn about boat safety while working on the Mississippi Sound. For instance, rules stipulating that running lights were mandatory for their boats were new to the Vietnamese. Through education and multicultural meetings, such problems were addressed and resolved.[30]

In order to prepare for citizenship, many Vietnamese attended classes sponsored by the Catholic Social and Community Services of Biloxi and funded by the federal government, just as earlier immigrants had done 50 years before. Also, in the 1970s, the Catholic Social Services and Migration and Refugee Center facilitated assimilation of the Vietnamese into American culture. Located in the old 1933 Sacred Heart Academy behind the Cathedral of the Nativity of the Blessed Virgin Mary on Howard Avenue, this center offered services to aid the immigrants' adjustment into their new environment and to help them in finding housing, employment, and medical assistance.[31]

Vietnamese businesses also began opening in Point Cadet. Groceries offering ethnic Vietnamese foods, hairdressers, insurance agencies, and restaurants appeared in the once Slavic-French neighborhood.[32] Point Cadet eastward to the Back Bay of Biloxi became a tricultural kaleidoscope of foods and peoples. At the turn of the twenty-first century, Kim Long's restaurant and the Vietnamese French Bakery served traditional Vietnamese foods while adapting to American culture. Two of the most popular centerpieces for local parties continue to be the French bread alligator or crab created by the Vietnamese owners of the French bakery. The vibrant mixture of Vietnamese and American cultures is also evident during the Christmas season as a Buddha statue on Oak Street is traditionally dressed with Christmas lights. Like its predecessors in Biloxi, the Vietnamese culture cannot exist wholly intact. Concessions and adaptations inevitably occur as cultures now mix in the Point Cadet-Back Bay regions, each molding Biloxi's ethnicity.

The seafood industry is at the heart of Biloxi's culture mix as it has been in other coastal regions. Changes in this one industry affected the entire city, not just the fisheries. Three cultures created one fabric in Biloxi: Slavonians, Acadians, and Vietnamese, each adapting and conforming yet maintaining cultural identity within one industry. Local ethnic festivals, such as the Blessing of the Fleet or the Vietnamese New Year Celebration and other long-held customs and traditions, continue to highlight the wide cultural net that these three groups cast over Biloxi.

The Last Daughter *of* Davis Ridge:

Mullet fishermen in their camp on Shackleford Banks, North Carolina, ca. 1880, George Brown Goode, ed., *The Fisheries and Fishery Industries of the United States* (Washington, D.C.,1884-1887), sect. 5, vol. 2. (G.W. Blunt White Library, Mystic Seaport)

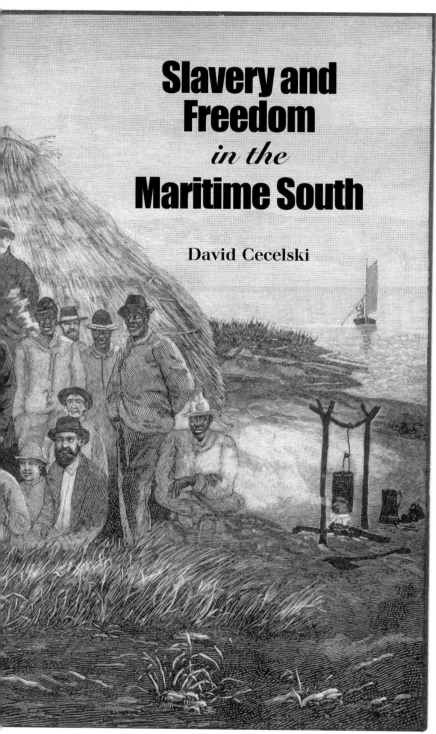

Slavery and
Freedom
in the
Maritime South

David Cecelski

When I pass the old clam house between Smyrna and Williston, I always glance east across Jarrett Bay to Davis Ridge. You will go that way if you drive Highway 70 across the broad salt marshes of Carteret County to catch the Cedar Island ferry to the Outer Banks. Most passers-by admire the beautiful vistas across Core Sound and look for the wild ponies grazing along the Cape Lookout National Seashore and the Cedar Island National Wildlife Refuge. Some travelers wander through the old seaside villages, such as Harkers Island, that are renowned for their boatbuilding, fishing, and seafaring heritages. Few coastal visitors know that the secluded hammock of Davis Ridge was once an extraordinary fishing community founded by liberated slaves. Nobody has lived at "the Ridge" since 1933, yet the legend of those African-American fishermen, whalers, and boatbuilders still echoes among the elderly people in the maritime communities between North River and Cedar Island that locals call "Downeast."

This writer had heard of Davis Ridge when I was growing up 25 miles west. As a historian, I searched for the history of those black Downeasterners. There was much ardor in the search, but little success. Perhaps all record of them had been lost. There was no trace of the people of Davis Ridge in history books. When exploring Davis Ridge by boat and on foot, one will find only an old cemetery in a live oak grove surrounded by salt marsh and, only a few yards away, Core Sound and Jarrett Bay. All the documents in research libraries, archives, and museums yielded only tantalizing clues to the community's past. The best sources seemed to be a few, mostly secondhand recollections from elderly people who had grown up in fishing villages not far from Davis Ridge. At last, after much reading, this writer stumbled upon a tape-recorded interview with Nannie Davis Ward in a storage pantry at the North Carolina Maritime Museum in Beaufort. Most success in historical research comes from persistence and hard work; finding Ward's interview was an undeserved act of grace.

Folklorists Michael and Debbie Luster had interviewed Ward only a couple of years before her death in 1988. At that time, Ward was apparently the last living soul to have grown up at Davis Ridge. A retired seamstress and cook, she was born at the Ridge in 1911. Ward was blind by the time the Lusters interviewed her, but she had a strong memory and a firm voice. When one listens to her eloquent words, a vivid portrait of her childhood home takes shape. Her story fills in an important part of the history of the African-American maritime peoples who inhabited the coastal villages and fishing camps of North Carolina before the Civil War. It is only the story of one community, Davis Ridge, but it speaks to the broader experience of the black watermen and women who came out of slavery and continued to work on the water.

When Nannie Davis Ward was a child, Davis Ridge was an all-black community on a wooded knoll, or small island, on the eastern shore of Jarrett Bay, not far from Core Sound and Cape Lookout. A great salt marsh separated the Ridge from the mainland to the north, which was known as Davis Shore. Davis Island was just to the south. A hurricane later cut a channel between Davis Ridge and Davis Island, but in Nannie's grandparents' day you could walk from one to the other.

The founders of Davis Ridge had been among many free-black and slave watermen at Core Sound before the Civil War. By itself, the piloting village of Portsmouth—on the northern tip of Core Banks—had a population of 110 slaves in 1800, nearly all of them engaged in maritime trades. There, slave crews piloted seagoing vessels through Ocracoke Inlet, lightered their cargo, and then guided them to distant seaports on the far side of Albemarle and Pamlico Sounds. Their slave neighbors at Shell Castle Island, a shoal at Ocracoke Inlet, ranged up and down the Outer Banks with their nets in a commercial fishery for jumping mullet and bottlenosed dolphins. Looking beyond the Outer Banks, along the Albemarle Sound, prodigious gangs of black fishermen wielded mile-and-a-half-long seines in what was the largest herring fishery in North America. Nearby, on the Roanoke River, solitary slave bateauxmen dared harrowing rapids and racing currents to transport tobacco from the foothills of the Blue Ridge Mountains all the way to seaports. In every port, slave stevedores trundled cargo on and off vessels, while shipyard workers in bondage turned out some of the sweetest-sailing juniper and white-oak boats anywhere, and of course caulked and rebuilt older vessels to stave off the steady rot that plagued them. Still other slave watermen hawked firewood to steamers anchored on the Cape Fear at night;

rafted lumber on the Lower Neuse River; poled shingle-laden flat-boats out of the Great Dismal Swamp; guided duck-hunting parties along the freshwater marshes of Currituck Sound; tonged for oysters on frigid winter days; shoveled coal in the sweltering firerooms of steamships; and manned the sloops and schooners on which the inland trade of North Carolina relied. This was the maritime culture out of which Nannie Davis Ward's people came.

Ward's family was typical of the African American families along the Lower Banks. They were skilled maritime laborers with a seafaring heritage. They had family roots in the West Indies and had black, white, and Native American ancestry. They moved seasonally from fishery to fishery, working on inshore waters, rarely on the open sea. Like so many of their predecessors, they also had a history of slave resistance. Nannie Ward's mother, who identified herself as Native American, had grown up on Bogue Banks, a 26-mile-long barrier island west of Beaufort, and her mother's grandfather had evidently been a sailor in bondage aboard a French sailing vessel. According to Ward, that great-grandfather had escaped from his French master while in port at New Bern and had been raised in the family of a white waterman at Harkers Island, ten miles west of Davis Ridge.

It was Sutton Davis, Ward's paternal grandfather, who first settled Davis Ridge. As a slave, Sutton Davis had belonged to a small planter and shipbuilder named Nathan Davis at Davis Island. Sutton Davis had been a master boatbuilder and carpenter. According to his granddaughter, he had learned the boatbuilding trade at a Wilmington shipyard owned by a member of the white Davis family, then moved back to Davis Island. Family lore on one side of the white Davis family holds that Nathan was Sutton's father. Nannie Davis Ward did not address that question in her interview, except to note that Sutton and his children were very light-skinned.

When Union troops captured Beaufort and New Bern in 1862, Sutton Davis led the Davis Island slaves to freedom. They rowed a small boat across Jarrett Bay to the fishing village of Smyrna, then fled to Union-occupied territory on the outskirts of New Bern. After the war, some of the former slaves founded the North River community, a few miles outside of Beaufort, but in 1865 Sutton

Davis bought four acres at Davis Ridge. Nathan Davis sold him the property for the sort of low price usually reserved for family. Sutton Davis and his children eventually acquired 220 more acres at Davis Ridge.

The number of black Downeasterners declined sharply after the Civil War, but Davis Ridge remained a stronghold of the African American maritime culture that had thrived along Core Sound. Nearly all of Nannie Davis Ward's relatives worked on the water. Her grandfather Sutton, of course, was a fisherman and boat-builder. Her mother's father, a free black named Samuel Windsor, became a legendary fisherman and whaler at Shackleford Banks, the nine-mile-long barrier island just east of Beaufort. (Sam Windsor's Lump is still a Shackleford landmark.) Her father, Elijah, owned a fish house. Her great-uncle Palmer was a seafarer and sharpie captain. Her great-uncle Adrian was captain of the fishing boat *Belford*. Another great-uncle, Proctor, was a waterman who lived at Quinine Point, the northwest corner of Davis Ridge. Many other kinsmen became stalwarts in the Beaufort menhaden fleet, which rose in the late nineteenth and early twentieth centuries into the state's most important saltwater fishery. During its heyday, black watermen dominated the menhaden fishery, which had black leadership earlier than any other local industry. Out of Nannie Davis Ward's family came the menhaden industry's first African American captains.

Sutton Davis and his 13 children themselves operated one of the first successful menhaden factories in North Carolina, long before the industry's boom in Beaufort. He built two fishing boats, the *Mary E. Reeves* and the *Shamrock*. His sons worked the boats while his daughters dried and pressed the menhaden—known locally as "shad" or "pogie"—to sell as fertilizer and oil.

"Men should have been doing it," Ward explained, "but he didn't have them there, so the girls had to fill in for them." In fact, Ward pointed out, at Davis Ridge, "the girls did a lot of farm working, factory work too."

The black families at Davis Ridge were what local historian Norman Gillikin in Smyrna calls "saltwater farmers": the old-time Downeasterners who lived by both fishing and farming. They hawked oysters across Jarrett Bay and raised hogs, sheep, and cattle. They grew corn for the animals and sweet "roasting ears" for themselves. At night they spun homegrown cotton into cloth. Their gardens were full of collard greens and, as Ward recalled vividly, "sweet potatoes as big as your head." They worked hard and prospered.

Other times, Sutton Davis augmented his children's labor by hiring fishing hands from Craven Corner, an African American community 30 miles west. Craven Corner had been settled in the eighteenth century by free blacks who had been granted land and freedom as a reward for their service in the Revolutionary War. According to local oral tradition, many had intermarried with the descendants of the Native American survivors of the Tuscarora War of 1711-1713. Over the generations, African Americans at Craven Corner had earned a strong reputation for a fierce independence and for being excellent watermen and artisans. One does not have to stretch one's imagination to see them fitting into the fishing life at Davis Ridge.

Davis Ridge was a proud, independent community. When Nannie Ward was growing up there in the 1910s and 1920s, seven families—all kin to Sutton Davis—lived at the Ridge. They sailed across Jarrett Bay to a Smyrna gristmill to grind their corn and to a Williston grocery to barter fish for coffee and sugar, but mainly relied on their own land and labor. They conducted business with their white neighbors at Davis Shore or across Jarrett Bay by barter and by trading chores. "You didn't know what it was to pay bills," Ward reminisced.

While the Davis Ridge men worked away at Core Banks mullet camps or chased menhaden into Virginia waters, the island women cared for farms and homes. They gathered tansy, sassafras, and other wild herbs for medicines and seasoning. They collected yaupon leaves in February, chopped them into small pieces, and dried them to make tea. In May, they sheared the sheep. Nannie Ward's grandmother spun and wove the wool. They produced, Ward explained, "everything they used."

Davis Ridge was a remote knoll, but Ward could not remember a day of loneliness or boredom. She told how two Beaufort men-hadenmen, William Henry Fulcher and John Henry, used to visit and play music on her front porch. "We enjoyed ourselves on the island," Ward said. "There wasn't a whole lot of things to do, but we enjoyed people. We visited each other."

The camaraderie of black and white neighbors around Davis Ridge was still striking to Nannie Ward half a century later. For most black coastal Carolinians, the 1910s and 1920s were years of hardship and fear. White citizens enforced racial segregation at gunpoint. Blacks who tried to climb above "their place" invited harsh reprisals. The Ku Klux Klan marched by the hundreds in coastal communities as nearby as Morehead City, and word went out in several fishing communities–including Knotts Island, Stumpy Point, and Atlantic–that a black man might not live long if he lingered after dark.

Davis Ridge was somehow different. Black and white families often worked, socialized, and worshiped together. "The people from Williston would come over to our island," Ward said of school recitals and plays, "and we'd go over to their place." Sutton Davis's home, in particular, was a popular meeting place. Hymn singers of both races visited his home at Davis Ridge to enjoy good company and the finest pipe organ around Jarrett Bay.

Ward even recalled a white midwife staying with black families at Davis Ridge when a child was about to be born, a simple act of kindness and duty that turned racial conventions of the day upside down. This may seem a trivial thing, but it was quite the opposite. A coastal midwife had to move into an expectant mother's home well before her due date or risk not being in attendance at the birth because of the time required to travel to and from the island. The midwife stayed for the child's birth, then tended to mother and child–and sometimes the cooking and house work–until the mother was recovered fully. Taking care of those duties, a midwife could easily spend two or three weeks living in the mother's household. In the American South during the Age of Jim Crow, it was not unusual at all for a black midwife to serve a white family in that capacity; the arrangement was entirely consistent with a traditional role of black women serving as maids and nannies in white homes. But to reverse the arrangement was unheard of. The white South simply did not allow one of its own to serve a black woman. Even more fundamental to the complex racial landscape of the day, a white woman could never stay the night under a black man's roof, that being a breech of the sexual code that was at the heart of Jim Crow. The daily conduct of blacks and whites at Davis Ridge would have caused riots, lynching, or banishment in most Southern places, including coastal towns 20 miles away.

Similarly, in the 1950s and 1960s, many white ministers across the American South lost their jobs for inviting black choirs to sing at a church revival. Yet the Davis Ridge choir sang at revivals at the Missionary Baptist church at Davis Shore two generations before the civil rights movement. An old legend even tells how, in 1871, black and white worshippers rushed from a prayer meeting and together made a daring rescue of the crew and cargo of a ship, the *Pontiac*, wrecked at Cape Lookout.

The work culture of mullet fishing on the barrier islands near Davis Ridge both reflected and reinforced this blurring of conventional racial lines. Every autumn all or most of the Davis Ridge men joined interracial mulleting gangs of four to thirty men tending seines, gillnets, and dragnets along the beaches between Ocracoke Island and Bogue Banks. During the 1870s and 1880s, that stretch of coastline supported the largest mullet fishery in the United States. More than 30 vessels carried the salted fish out of Beaufort and Morehead City, and the Atlantic and North Carolina Railroad transported such large quantities that for generations local people referred to it as the "Old Mullet Road."

Out on those remote islands, black and white mullet fishermen lived, dined, and worked together all autumn, temporarily sharing a life beyond the pale of the stricter racial barriers ashore. They worked side-by-side handling sails and hauling nets, and every man's gain depended on his crew's collective sailing and fishing skills. For most, a lot was riding on the mullet season. Local fishermen were a hand-to-mouth lot, and mulleting was one of the few fisheries that promised barter for the flour, cornmeal, and other staples necessary to fill a winter pantry, to say nothing of putting aside a little for Christmas or for a bolt of calico that might save their wives a fortnight of late-night weaving. Every fisherman hoped for the strongest crew possible, and nobody worked the mullet nets or knew how to survive the vicious storms on the barrier islands better than the men from Davis Ridge. On those secluded islands, away from the prying eyes of the magistrates of Jim Crow, a man's race could start to seem a little less important. Work customs reflected this camaraderie and interdependence. Mullet fishermen traditionally worked on a "share system," granting equal parts of their profits to every hand no matter his race. (Owners of boats and nets earned extra shares.) Often they also voted by shares to settle work-related decisions. These were the sort of working conditions that might attract even the independent-minded souls of Davis Ridge to work alongside their white counterparts.

This fraternity of black and white fishermen on the islands off Davis Ridge comes across clearly in a stunning engraving of a Shackleford Banks mullet camp. The photograph on which this engraving is based was taken in about 1880 by R. Edward Earll, a fishery biologist who was visiting the local mulleting beaches as part of the United States Fish Commission's monumental survey of all of the nation's fisheries. When looking at the engraving closely, what stands out immediately are the equal numbers of black and white fishermen, their intermingled pose, close quarters, obvious familiarity—one might even say chuminess—and the unclear lines of authority. All were entirely foreign to the standard racial attitudes of the American South in that day. It's one of the most extraordinary portraits ever made in the Age of Jim Crow, and another photograph or drawing like it may not exist. One never sees anything close to that intimacy and equality in the photographs of black and white workers in cotton mills, lumber camps, coal mines, or agricultural fields, much less in the trades or professions. The notion of blacks and whites sharing a fish camp of African American design stretches the imagination even farther. A mullet fisherman from Davis Ridge may, in fact, have built the camp in this photograph. Sallie Salter, who lived near the Ridge from 1805 to 1903, recalled for her grandson that Proctor Davis "lived in a rush camp" at Davis Ridge, and later moved closer to her family at Salter Creek "and built another rush camp, and lived in it for a long time."

It is important not to exaggerate the racial harmony around Davis Ridge. Not a crossroads in the American South escaped the ugliness of racial oppression. Certainly Davis Ridge did not. After the statewide white supremacy campaigns of 1898 and 1900, local whites fostered an atmosphere of racial intimidation that increasingly drove African Americans out of other parts of Downeast, as well as discouraged any new black settlement in the fishing villages east of North River. For years, a hand-scrawled sign at the town limits of Atlantic, a fishing village 15 miles from Davis Ridge, read: "No Niggers After Dark." As little as 50 years ago, no blacks lived anywhere Downeast, and, like anybody that grew up where I did, I often heard the admonition that African Americans could work days in the Downeast clam houses or oyster shucking sheds, but could never spend the night safely. During that period, this writer was on a club field trip to one of my teachers' homes at Harkers Island. The teacher, a native of Downeast, had the one African-American girl in the club lie on the floor of her car as soon as she drove across the North River Bridge. My teacher did not have to explain why. Seen in this light, Davis Ridge was an island in more than one sense; as the rest of Downeast grew whiter and whiter after the Civil War, this remote knoll was increasingly seen as a last redoubt of African-American independence and self-sufficiency. White fishermen could look across Jarrett Bay and refer to the *Mary E. Reeves* or the *Shamrock* as "the nigger boats," as Downeast oldtimers called them, but Sutton Davis's clan still had one of the only menhaden boats Downeast and the skills to make good money with it.

That was the heart of the matter. Sutton Davis and his descendants could not remove themselves from the white supremacy pervasive in the American South, but they had at least two advantages that most black Southerners could only dream of: land and a fair chance to make a living. And, unlike the rest of the Jim Crow South, the broad waters of Core Sound could not so easily be segregated into separate and unequal sections. Self-reliant, in peonage to no one, the African Americans at Davis Ridge joined their white neighbors as rough equals in a common struggle to make a living from the sea.

Ward left Davis Ridge in 1925. She first went to Beaufort to attend high school, then moved to South Carolina and New York. While she was gone, the great 1933 hurricane laid waste to the island's homes and fields. The Ridge was deserted when she returned in 1951. No African Americans resided anywhere Downeast by that time.

"I still loved the island," Ward told the Lusters only a few years before she died in Beaufort. "When you grow up there from a child, you learn all the things in the island, you learn how to survive. You learn everything."

On the recording, one can hear a low, wistful sigh and a deep yearning in her voice. "We were surrounded by so many good things that I don't get anymore, that I never did get again" It is clear that she was not speaking merely of roasted mullet and fresh figs.

She was silent a moment. Then, with a laugh, she exclaimed, "I'd like to be there right now."

"Rebecca, woman from Africa, was enslaved in Chilmark, but died a free woman in this place," reads this plaque on the African American Heritage Trail at Martha's Vineyard, Massachusetts.
(Elaine Cawley Weintraub photo)

"Where Were All the Black People Then?"

The History of the African American Heritage Trail of Martha's Vineyard

Elaine Cawley Weintraub

The history of a community becomes lost, or distorted, when recorded through the perspective of the dominant culture. For this reason, people of color are absent from the larger American narrative in many cases. Where they are mentioned, their experience is described from the perspective of the power structure.[1] Throughout the United States, the history most often preserved and recounted is the conqueror's story. Therefore, the lives of people of color were only recorded, if at all, in relation to their interaction with the dominant culture. By being excluded from the history of America, their contributions were ignored. What is the impact of that exclusion? Could it be "a moment of psychic disequilibrium, as if you looked into a mirror and saw nothing?" The result is that history may be forgotten, and lost.[2]

A case in point is the African American people on the Island of Martha's Vineyard, Massachusetts. The achievements of people of color were not included in the Island narrative, and they had lost their history and their community heroes.

The philosophy that inspired a disregard for the experiences of people of color was deeply rooted in racist attitudes that sought to undermine and replace the cultural values deemed to be uncivilized. Ronald Takaki, in his examination of dominant culture attitudes in the United States, attributes the white, Anglo-Saxon attitude of racial superiority to the English, whom he believes developed that attitude during their conquest of Ireland in the twelfth century. That concept of racial and cultural superiority conditioned the behavior of the European settlers toward the Native Americans when they encountered them in the New World. Attitudes of racial superiority remained pervasive thoughout the history of the United States.[3]

Despite the lack of a recorded history, it is possible to pursue official documentation to piece together the presence of an individual in history. It is much more difficult, however, to piece together a narrative of that person's life. When the history of a community is lost, what is available to us is incomplete and even misleading. Peoples who are dominated do not have ready access to publications and other media outlets to tell their story; for that reason, they lose their community heroes, and thus, their own history is threatened. Howard Zinn described this phenomenon, saying: "The idea of saviors has been built into the entire culture, beyond politics. We have learned to look to stars, leaders, experts in every field, thus surrendering our own strength, threatening our own ability, obliterating our own selves."[4]

The evidence of a rich African American history on Martha's Vineyard was never compiled into published reports. I heard stories of the existence of an African American whaling captain, evidence of the institution of enslavement was available in the form of probated wills, and there was a small community of people of color whose story had not been told.

When I began to research the African American history of Martha's Vineyard, the initial research was published in the *New England Journal of History* in 1993. I continued to publish and present my research findings at academic conferences, but I was aware that this history was still not reaching the people for whom it meant the most, the people of the Island. To help remedy this problem, the African American Heritage Trail was established.

The African American Heritage Trail consists of a series of identified sites commemorating the history of people of color on Martha's Vineyard. There is also a nonprofit corporation, founded by myself and the vice president of the Martha's Vineyard chapter of the N.A.A.C.P., called The African American Heritage Trail History Project. The mission of the corporation is to research, disseminate information, and educate the community of Martha's Vineyard about the African American history of their island.

Several historic sites have been identified, and plaques celebrating the existence and achievements of individual people of color have been placed at each one. A brief history of people of color whose lives on Martha's Vineyard I researched has been published under the title *African American Heritage Trail of Martha's Vineyard.* The sophomore history classes of Martha's Vineyard Regional High School assisted in archival research for the Heritage Trail, in gathering oral histories, in doing art work, and in landscaping and site maintenance under my direction and guidance.

The African American Heritage Trail History Project is an action research project. Action research is defined as "a form of collective self-reflective inquiry to improve the rationality and justice of their own social practices, as well as their understanding of these practices, and the situations in which these practices are carried out."[5]

In keeping with the principles of action research,

reflection is a vital part of the researcher's role. To reflect on practice is absolutely necessary in order to achieve critical consciousness. If valid transformative solutions are to be found, they do not emanate from the researcher, but from the shared reflective experience. As Brookfield suggests, reflection becomes critical when it has two distinctive purposes. The first is to understand how considerations of power undergird, frame, and distort educational processes and interactions. The second is to question assumptions and practices that seem to make our lives easier, but which actually work against our own best, long-term interests.[6]

It is impossible to separate one's experience from the reflective process. To be critically aware, one must understand not only the structures of power and domination, but also the role one plays in perpetuating those structures. When I speak for myself, I am participating in the creation and reproduction of discourses through which my own, and other selves are constituted. The category of voice can only be constituted in differences, and it is in and through these multiple layers of meaning that students are positioned and position themselves in order to be the subject rather than merely the object of history.[7]

I began researching the history of the African American community of Martha's Vineyard in 1989. I was inspired to do so by the complete lack of any reference to that history in the school where I was employed. The catalyst actually to begin the work was a small boy who asked me, "Where were all the Black people then?" His question began my journey.

The original work was archival in that I explored old newspapers, shipping logs, reports, obituaries, bills of sale, probated wills, and court records. I succeeded in documenting the life of an African American whaling captain, William A. Martin, the details of whose life had become shrouded in obscurity. Through searching census records, wedding certificates, and court records, I managed to uncover and document the lives of three remarkable women of his family.

This research project followed the format of examining the specific issue of enslavement and the lives of people of color whose experiences had not been documented or recorded.

I began to research the question of enslavement on Martha's Vineyard after I found a copy of a bill of sale that documented the sale of a ten-year-old Negro boy, Peter, by Zacheus Mayhew of Edgartown to Ebenezer Hatch of Falmouth. The document was part of a huge mass of uncatalogued papers at the Vineyard Museum. The date of the transaction was June 19, 1747. I pursued this line of inquiry by reading an article that had been published in the *Dukes County Intelligencer* in August 1991. The article by Jacqueline Holland included a paragraph describing the inclusion of enslaved people in the wills of certain of the founding families of Martha's Vineyard. I searched the archives of the Probate Department of the Town Clerk's Office and read several wills where enslaved people were listed as part of the inventory of property.

Having established the existence of enslavement on Martha's Vineyard, I began a detailed study of how that institution was established in the Massachusetts Bay Colony. I read widely among the diaries and journals of early English settlers in the colony, particularly the work of Samuel Sewell, whose sermon, "The Selling of Joseph," published in 1700, is considered the first definitive anti-slavery statement among the settlers. "Liberty," he stated, "is the real value unto life and one ought not part with it themselves or deprive others of it, but upon mature consideration."[8]

What emerged from my investigation is a rich history of African American people. That history eventually came to be told by a series of plaques placed at specific sites on the Heritage Trail. The African American Heritage Trail has seven dedicated sites. They are described here with a brief history of the research process that identified them.

William A. Martin, African American Whaling Captain

I had been told that there had been a "black whaling captain on Chappaquiddick," a small adjoining island considered part of the Town of Edgartown. I interviewed several older members of the Chappaquiddick community, who told me that this man had lived in the Chappaquiddick Plantation, a Native American reservation. His name, they told me, was Captain Martin. The next step was to substantiate the existence of that plantation and find population records. Research at the Widener Library at Harvard revealed a report to the governor and council by John Milton Earle in 1861 relating to the "condition of the Indians." Attached to the report was a list describing the ethnicity, occupation, and whereabouts of each person. There was the name I had been given: William A. Martin, described as a "colored foreigner." I searched the records of the whaling ships owned by Samuel Osborn of Edgartown. These records had been compiled by Alexander Starbuck and published in *History of the American Whale Fishery* and a later addendum. They confirmed that William Martin had commanded several whaling vessels in the latter years of the whaling industry. I was able to find details of all of his voyages and the amount of sperm oil each trip had yielded. As master of the 86-ton schooner *Emma Jane*, he made a voyage to the Atlantic whaling grounds. The voyage began on October 9, 1883, and he returned on March 27, 1884, with 140 barrels of sperm oil. He commanded the *Golden City* out of New Bedford in 1878, and in 1887 he commanded the *Eunice H. Adams* out of Edgartown. His long and successful career spanned more than 30 years.[9]

I contacted every whaling museum in the Massachusetts area to research the question of logbooks. Generally, the first mate kept the log of a whaling voyage. If I could find logs kept by William Martin I could document his earlier career and William Martin's own description of his journey, written in his own hand. The Kendall Whaling Museum did have a logbook for the voyage of the *Europa* from Edgartown in 1857, and William Martin was the keeper of the log. The logbook was on microfilm, but I was able to establish that Martin had remarkable artistic skills. Several drawings of whales decorated the pages, as was customary, but of more interest was a picture on the first page of the house on Chappaquiddick Island known as the Martin house, where he lived after his marriage to Sarah Brown. The house on Chappaquiddick was part of the Indian Plantation and was the residence of Sarah Brown's Native American family. The drawing made by William Martin is immediately recognizable. The date of this voyage preceded his marriage to Sarah, and the logbook was in poor condition, but I was able to decipher the words written above the drawing of the house.

Farewell to thee for a time
Days' lingering sun is over
This heart will never awaken it
to one bright moment more the hope
.... cherished here within
day by day through life's flow.[10]

This writing gave valuable insight into William Martin's life and demonstrated his affection for his future wife and the place in which she lived. Research in the archives of the Genealogy Project in New Bedford revealed a copy of William Martin's marriage certificate.

The census report for 1850 revealed that William Martin then lived with his mother, Rebecca Michael, and grandmother, Nancy Michael. The residence they shared no longer exists.

Research at the *Vineyard Gazette* offices turned up a tribute to William Martin on his fiftieth wedding anniversary, published by the newspaper in 1907. The paper called him a respected "whaling man" and expressed sympathy for the fact that he was now a "paralytic."

The African American Heritage Trail History Project published a brief biography of Captain Martin in a booklet to which students at the Martha's Vineyard Regional High School contributed material. One student wrote an essay reflecting on the question of why Captain Martin's gravestone, though elaborate, faces away from the other graves in the cemetery. Another drew a portrait of Captain Martin from archival descriptions (there are no photographs of him). Although wide publicity has been given to William Martin in the last five years, no plaque has yet been placed either on the Martin house or in the Chappaquiddick graveyard.

Rebecca Martin, also known as Michael and Francis

Research into the vital records kept in New Bedford showed that on his marriage certificate, William Martin gave the name of only one parent, Rebecca Francis. An examination of Edgartown's vital records showed that Rebecca Martin married John Francis in 1831. Her son had been born in 1829, but I found no record of a marriage prior to the one with John Francis. The records of the Dukes County Jail in Edgartown show that in 1820 Rebecca Michael had been imprisoned twice for periods of twenty days for theft and non-payment of debts. The informant against her on both occasions was her mother, Nancy Michael. Her age in these records was given as eleven, and her year of birth as 1809. An article about the journals of Jeremiah Pease published in the *Dukes County Intelligencer* included an entry dated October 29, 1854: "Rebecca, a coloured woman died. She was the daughter of Nancy Michael aged about fifty years. She died about 8:00 a.m."[11] The Heritage Trail History Project has placed a bench at the Eastville Cemetery, where it is believed that Rebecca is buried. A plaque on the bench bears the inscription: "Rebecca Michael, 1809-1854, Nobody knows the trouble I've seen." This wording was chosen because it seemed appropriate to her life and because it is an old African American spiritual song. The song was among the spirituals written down and saved for posterity by Harry Burleigh, a summer resident on Martha's Vineyard for many years. The Eastville Cemetery is an abandoned cemetery formerly used for vagrants, mariners from away, and people of color. It is now recognized as a site on the African American Heritage Trail.

Nancy Michael, African American Woman of Power

In 1851, William Martin's grandmother, Nancy Michael, had been the cause of a legal battle between two Island towns. The battle had focused on the issue of whether Nancy Michael had ever been enslaved. I researched court records and established that the Town of Edgartown was suing the Town of Tisbury, alleging that Tisbury was responsible for the financial maintenance of Nancy Michael, a public pauper. The legal case was based on the fact that Nancy Michael had been enslaved in the Town of Tisbury and was therefore its financial responsibility. A deposition was given during that trial by an elderly woman, Remember Cooper, a former neighbor of Nancy Michael's mother, Rebecca. When asked by counsel for the Town of Edgartown if Nancy Michael had been born into slavery, Remember Cooper replied that she had been born on the estate of Colonel Cornelius Bassett in Chilmark. Research at the Dukes County Registry of Probate showed that Colonel Bassett's will listed "Nancy, aged 7" in the inventory of his property sold at the time of his death in 1779 and recorded that she had been sold to Joseph Allen of Tisbury.

A court action was taken by the Town of Edgartown in 1813 against the Town of Tisbury to force Tisbury to pay for the upkeep of one of Nancy Michael's children born about 1810. Edgartown prevailed in this issue.

Research in the Dukes County Registry of Deeds showed that Nancy Michael "spinster, sister and only surviving heir to James Michael" conveyed land inherited from her brother to Isaiah D. Pease of Edgartown for $10.00 on December 20, 1819. This finding does not suggest that Nancy was not enslaved, as the Commonwealth of Massachusetts allowed enslaved people to inherit and sell property.

The court documents for the hearing in 1851 between Edgartown and Tisbury concerning support for Nancy Michael state that following her sale to Joseph Allen in 1779, he "held and used her as a slave for a series of years." It is further stated that "she fell into distress in Edgartown in 1812." The verdict in the 1851 hearing was taken for the Town of Tisbury, which admitted that Nancy Michael had been enslaved there, but claimed that her enslavement had been illegal because the Commonwealth of Massachusetts had abolished slavery in 1788.

A search of the archives of the *Vineyard Gazette* uncovered an obituary for Nancy Michael published on January 2, 1857. The obituary referred to her as unusually fond of children, and reminded the people of Edgartown that many of them had "at some time been indebted to her." The document then stated that Nancy Michael had "acquired great influence over some of our people, by many of whom she was looked upon as a witch. She professed to have the power of giving good or bad luck to those bound on long voyages. . . . In case of bad news from any vessel commanded by one who had defied her power, she was in ecstasies, and her fiendish spirit would at once take full control of her.

The obituary concluded: "May her good deeds live long in our remembrance, and her evil be interred with her bones." A plaque has been placed at the waterfront in Edgartown to celebrate Nancy's life. It reads: "Nancy Michael, 1773-1856, a most singular woman."

Rebecca from Africa

I read through the depositions given in the court case between the towns of Edgartown and Vineyard concerning the status of Nancy Michael and found a reference to Nancy Michael's mother, Rebecca. According to a deposition given by Remember Cooper, Nancy Michael's mother had been "Beck," a "Guinea woman" and a slave. Asked how she knew that "Beck" was a slave, she replied: "She was called a slave all the time. . . he used to whip her like a dog. I have heard Colonel Bassett's boys call her a slave all the time."[12]

The same deposition stated that Rebecca (Beck) had lived for a number of years with a man named Elisha Amos, who was referred to as an Indian man. Speaking of Rebecca's relationship with Elisha

Amos, Remember Cooper recalled: "I never knew they were married, they separated and got together again and he died then. She lived most of the time with Colonel Bassett. The place where Amos died was about five or six miles from Colonel Bassett's."

A search for supporting documentation in the Dukes County Probate Office revealed Elisha Amos's will in which he left his house to his beloved wife, Rebecca, for as long as she shall live. Upon her death, his property was to revert to his nephews. A title search of Mr. Amos's property in the Dukes County Registry of Deeds found that he had bought many pieces of land over the years, amassing a considerable amount of property. The Heritage Trail History Project has placed a plaque near the property that Rebecca inherited from her husband, Elisha Amos. It reads: "Rebecca, woman from Africa, was enslaved in Chilmark, but died a free woman in this place."

Shearer Cottage, Oak Bluffs

The Shearer Cottage is the first African American-owned inn on Martha's Vineyard that was open to people of color. It was owned and operated by Charles and Henrietta Shearer. I interviewed two of the grandchildren of the Shearers and learned that Charles Shearer had been born into enslavement in Virginia. He was freed after the Civil War and was sent to the Hampton Institute where he became a teacher. He stayed there for twelve years, during which he met Henrietta Merchant, a Native American woman. Charles and Henrietta Shearer married and moved to Massachusetts, where Mr. Shearer became a waiter at the Parker House Hotel in Boston. Both were devout Baptists, and they came to Martha's Vineyard to attend meetings at the Baptist Revivalist Campground. They bought their house from the Baptist Tabernacle and originally operated it as a laundry. In the 1920s they opened the inn, which became a focus for affluent and well-known people of color. The guest book for the Shearer Cottage shows names of eminent African Americans such as Adam Clayton Powell, Harry Burleigh, and William Lewis. Though much of the information on the Shearer Cottage was given by the family, I was able to use the archives of the Registry of Deeds to find property deeds. The archives of the *Vineyard Gazette* contained many articles describing events at the Shearer Cottage. The

Shearer Cottage was the first site to be dedicated on the African American Heritage Trail of Martha's Vineyard.

John Saunders, African American Preacher

I learned about John Saunders through reading the diaries of Jeremiah Pease, edited by Railton. Mr. Pease spoke of John Saunders as a martyr because he had been murdered by Native American people while introducing Methodism to that community on the Chappaquiddick Plantation. A deposition given by Mr. Saunders's granddaughter, Mrs. Priscilla Freeman, is held at the Vineyard Museum. Mrs. Freeman described John Saunders as "pure African." She believed that her grandfather "preached with zeal and became acquainted with Jane Dimon and married with her which exasperated the Indians there on account of his African descent."

A large rock known as Pulpit Rock, in the Farm Neck area of Oak Bluffs, is believed to be where John Saunders preached. Pease noted that "John, being an exhorter, having it is understood held that position among his fellow slaves, preached occasionally to the people of color at Farm Neck."[13] A plaque has been placed near to Pulpit Rock dedicated to John Saunders. The wording reads: "John, being an exhorter, preached to the people of color at this place."

Multi-Racial Basketball Team at the Martha's Vineyard Regional High School (1970-72)

The most recent plaque dedicated by the African American Heritage Trail of Martha's Vineyard was the most controversial and generated the most excitement and interest in the Island community. It celebrates the achievements of a multi-racial basketball team at the Martha's Vineyard Regional High School during the early 1970s. The school principal agreed to the installation of the plaque, but suggested that the most appropriate site for it would be in the athletics area of the school. This is a remote area of the school used only by the athletes, and I resisted that placement. It was important that this plaque should be placed where it would be seen by everyone who entered the school. Even more important was that the placement of the plaque should allow students to see their family names displayed. I envisioned that the plaque would be a source of pride for students of color. The negotiations were lengthy, but agreement was reached and the plaque is situated in the entrance area of the school. It was dedicated by Amaury Bannister and Ronald Brown, two African American basketball players who had played with great distinction on the team.

CONCLUSION

This action research project follows the format of what Stringer calls look, think, and take action.[14] It involves the African American community and has had a transformative effect on the history curricula offered in the Martha's Vineyard Regional High School. In keeping with the key concepts of critical pedagogy, education has been used to address an inequity and make a meaningful transformation. There are now 13 plaques on Martha's Vineyard celebrating the achievements of the African American community. The booklet published by the African American Heritage Trail is sold in Island bookstores, and a mural painted by a student at the regional high school has been printed on T-shirts that are sold on the Island to publicize the work of the African American Heritage Trail of Martha's Vineyard. The goal now is to determine what the Heritage Trail means to our community and look for ways to enhance community education about African American history on the Island.

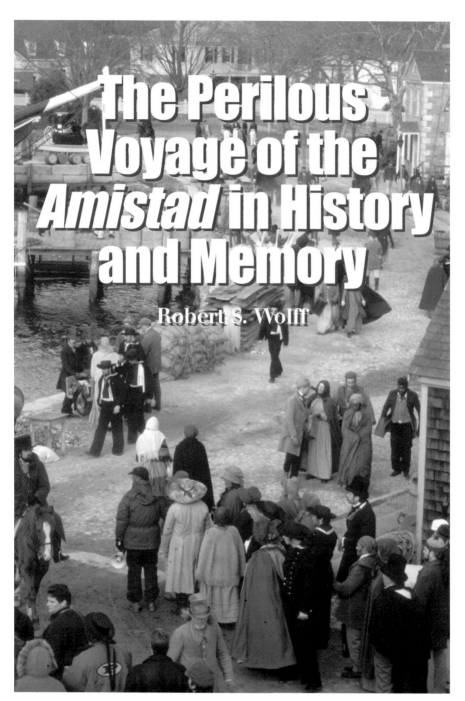

The Perilous Voyage of the *Amistad* in History and Memory

Robert S. Wolff

Costumed extras paraded the waterfront at Mystic Seaport during
the filming of Steven Spielberg's *Amistad* in 1997.
(Mystic Seaport, Mary Anne Stets photo)

Five years after the debut of Steven Spielberg's *Amistad*, the voyage of the *Amistad* story in history and popular memory remains perilous. Although the tale is most widely known through Spielberg's cinematic rendition, the story has also been popularized in the late twentieth century through works of historical fiction by William Owens, Barbara Chase-Riboud, Alexis Pate, David Pesci, and Karen Zeinert.[1] While historical inaccuracies appear to be inevitable in fictional representations of the past, both the film and the literary versions of the *Amistad* story are distorted not simply because they imagine the past or because their authors neglected to read appropriate historical documents, but rather because they fail to appreciate the ways in which historical documents offer narratives that are themselves constructed. In other words, a Hollywood film or novel without literary license would be nothing more than a documentary or textbook, yet they must still be held to an exacting historical standard. Does the fictional account substantially alter the historical meaning of the events it depicts? Both the Spielberg film and the historical fiction do so because they strip the *Amistad* story out of the appropriate historical context, namely the Atlantic World. Curmudgeonly readers may protest that no screenwriter or author should be held to such an expectation: after all, movie revenues come from American audiences who are more interested in a story about American history than in the nebulous category of the Atlantic World. To this it must be responded that, indeed, certain aspects of the *Amistad* story could be rendered within these parameters by, for example, looking at the effect of the *Amistad* cases on President Martin Van Buren's re-election campaign in 1840. Certain topics, however, can only be understood within an Atlantic World perspective, including: 1) the context of the Atlantic slave trade and the Middle Passage; 2) the role of slavery in nineteenth-century plantation economies; 3) race and the character of Northern abolition; and, 4) the role of admiralty law in the *Amistad* verdict. U.S. history provides a necessary but not sufficient context for the *Amistad*.

This article begins by providing an overview of the *Amistad* affair, highlighting the key moments, and providing a sense of chronology. Precisely because the analysis below criticizes the historical narrative provided by the fictionalized accounts, it is important to acknowledge that the narrative provided here is certainly subject to deconstruction as well. It is circumscribed to cover the events typically included in both historical and fictional works, thus providing a touchstone for the analysis that follows. The second major section explores Spielberg's *Amistad* in conjunction with the works of historical fiction to explore how the film's producers, screenwriters, and director produced their narrative. Since these accounts drew upon historical sources, the third section examines one example of how the antislavery activists constructed their own narrative in defense of the Africans, namely John Warner Barber's *A History of the Amistad Captives* (1840). The final section develops an Atlantic World perspective for the *Amistad* affair.

The story begins near present-day Sierra Leone in the spring of 1839, when several hundred enslaved Africans were forced onboard the *Tecora*, a Portuguese vessel, for the journey to Spanish Cuba and its sugar plantations. Once the *Tecora* arrived in Cuba, having evaded the British patrols that enforced the ban on the Atlantic slave trade, forty-nine of the men were sold to Jose Ruiz, while three girls and one boy were sold to Pedro Montes. Both slaveholders secured a passport (*trespasso*) that identified their property as *ladinos*, which in practice meant slaves born into slavery in the Americas. On June 28, they boarded the schooner *Amistad* in Havana for the coastal journey along Cuba's northern coast to Puerto Príncipe.

Onboard the schooner they joined the captain, Ramón Ferrer, and four crewmen (including two sailors, a cook named Celestino, and the cabin boy, Antonio). Several days into the journey, the captives escaped from the cargo hold and, armed with sugarcane knives they found among the goods stowed onboard, rose up, killing the captain and the cook. The two sailors abandoned ship and were presumed drowned. Once in command of the *Amistad*, the captives, led by Sengbe Pieh (Joseph Cinque), ordered Ruiz and Montes to steer the vessel back to Africa by sailing toward the sunrise. Placed in charge of navigating the vessel, however, Montes struggled to reach landfall, first in the Bahamas, and then by sailing north toward the coast of the United States. By late August, after making contact with a number of other vessels along the way, the *Amistad* appeared off the coast of Long Island, where the Africans dropped anchor and sent a boat ashore in search of provisions and water. Late on the 25th, the Africans met Henry Green and several of his friends. Green had heard stories about the schooner and hoped to take possession of it and sail to a nearby harbor in order to claim salvage. On the following morning, however, the *Amistad* was seized by the USS *Washington* and then sailed to the port of New London, Connecticut, where the naval officers hoped they (instead) would receive salvage on the vessel, its cargo, and the Africans they believed to be slaves.[2]

After the federal district court judge, Andrew T. Judson, presided over an initial hearing on board the *Washington* in New London harbor, the captives were placed in the custody of the U.S. marshal. He ordered the captives held until the next grand jury of the circuit court convened in September. In the meantime, the captives were held in the New Haven jail where they first encountered the abolitionists who became their staunchest allies in the their struggle for freedom. As both Bertram Wyatt-Brown and Howard Jones concluded, the *Amistad* affair provided a rallying point for abolitionists within the disparate wings of the movement. Whether they advocated immediate emancipation following the lines of William Lloyd Garrison or the more gradual path advocated by Lewis Tappan, all agreed that the captives should at once be returned to their native Africa.[3] They engaged prominent attorneys Roger Sherman Baldwin, Seth Staples, and Theodore Sedgwick to plead the captives' case. To raise money for the defense, Tappan, Joshua Leavitt, and Simeon Jocelyn formed the "Amistad Committee" which, in addition to fundraising duties, also publicized the captives' plight. With the assistance of Yale College professor Josiah W. Gibbs, the defense team identified two Africans, James Covey and Charles Pratt, who could speak Mende and therefore communicate directly with the captives. Prior to the opening of the circuit court on September 19, the Amistad Committee had learned the full details of the Africans' enslavement, transportation, and resale in Cuba and also about their uprising onboard the *Amistad.*

President Martin Van Buren and his cabinet, however, had decided in early September to support the claims of Ruiz, Montes, and the Spanish government. Attorney General Felix Grundy drafted an opinion that called upon the circuit court to release the ship, cargo, and the supposed slaves to Spain. Grundy argued that American courts had no judicial authority to inquire into the validity of documents issued to Ruiz and Montes by the Spanish government in Cuba. Nor were the captives to be considered and tried as pirates because, in the words of Howard Jones, the *Amistad* "was Spanish, belonged to Spaniards, was protected by Spanish papers and flag, and was moving from one Spanish port to another." In the eyes of Spanish law, the captives were themselves Spanish, and therefore any charges of murder or violations of the Spanish ban upon the Atlantic slave trade would have to be made in Spanish courts.[4]

On September 19, 1839, the circuit court convened in Hartford. While Judge Judson received salvage claims for the *Amistad* in district court proceedings, Judge Smith Thompson, the associate justice of the Supreme Court assigned to the Second Circuit, opened proceedings in what might best be described as a carnival-like atmosphere. As the captives awaited their fate, the New Haven jail charged admission to curiosity-seekers who wanted a glimpse of them. In Hartford, the hotels were booked and the courtroom packed. What the captives understood of their attorneys' legal strategies is unclear, but when Baldwin and the other attorneys for the captives sought a writ of habeas corpus for the three girls, the cleverness of the legal strategy eluded the girls entirely. As Howard Jones suggests, the abolitionists "could hardly have hoped for a stronger indictment of slavery than the spectacle of a United States marshal bringing in the three black girls, weeping with terror and desperately clutching the jailer's hands as he tried to calm them with pieces of fruit." In their bid to force the court to acknowledge the girls as persons under the law, the abolitionists failed to appreciate the emotional impact their appearance would have upon them.[5] On September 23, Thompson denied the motion for the writ, instructing parties to bring their claims to the district court. Judson then convened the district court, but only long enough to direct both sides to proceed to Long Island to establish the position of the *Amistad* when she was seized by the *Washington*. Should they have concluded that the *Amistad* was seized in a bay, harbor, or above the low-water mark on the Long Island coastline, then the cases would have fallen under the jurisdiction of New York.[6] In mid-October, Cinque and Fuliwa filed civil suits through their attorneys against Ruiz and Montes in New York, one in the court of common pleas and the other in superior court. No doubt to their great surprise, Ruiz and Montes were initially held in a New York jail on $1000 bond each. The courts ultimately released Montes, who fled back to Cuba, but Ruiz remained in custody for four months before posting a reduced bail of $250. Then he, too, departed for Cuba.[7]

After Judson concluded that the seizure of the *Amistad* had occurred at sea, the district court convened on November 19. Judge Judson confronted a variety of claims: Lieutenants Gedney and Meade for salvage; Henry Green also for salvage, claiming that he had saved the *Amistad* before the *Washington* appeared in sight; Ruiz and Montes for the return of their "cargo and slaves"; several other Spanish merchants who had purchased the cargo in the *Amistad's* hold; and U.S. District Attorney William Holabird for the American government, seeking to return the ship, cargo, and captives under the terms of treaties with Spain.[8] District court proceedings, which were postponed until January 7, 1840, provided the *Amistad* captives the first opportunity to appear in their own behalf. Sullivan Haley and Dwight Janes, both advocates for the captives, testified that at the initial inquiry onboard the *Washington*, Ruiz had acknowledged to Janes that only Antonio could speak Spanish because the others were from Africa. Then James Covey and Charles Pratt testified that all were indeed from Africa, and most were Mende. Professor Gibbs concurred. But the most riveting testimony came from Cinque, Grabeau, and Fuliwa, who described their enslavement in Africa and explained that their revolt on the *Amistad* occurred only after they had been whipped for stealing water and after the cook told them they would later be eaten. District Attorney William Holabird tried to convince Judson that Spanish law *in Cuba* allowed Africans smuggled into the island to become slaves legally. Moreover, since plantation slaves often continued to use their original languages daily, there was no way to tell if the *Amistad* captives were *ladinos* or *bozales* (born in Africa). In dramatic fashion, Judson ruled on January 8 that while Gedney and Meade were entitled to salvage on the ship and cargo, the captives had been illegally enslaved, transported to Cuba, and then sold to Ruiz and Montes. He ordered that the captives be placed in the government's charge for their return to Africa. After President Van Buren instructed Holabird to appeal the decision, the circuit court composed of Thompson and Judson affirmed Judson's ruling in May 1840, and the matter went before the Supreme Court.[9]

By the time that the Supreme Court heard the *Amistad* case, Martin Van Buren had lost his bid for re-election to William Henry

Harrison, and the Amistad Committee had persuaded former president John Quincy Adams to serve as lead counsel before the court. Adams, then serving as a representative to Congress from Massachusetts, had already provided numerous legal insights to Baldwin and the other counsel for the captives. When the Supreme Court convened in late February 1841, Attorney General Henry Gilpin reiterated the government's case: to borrow once again from Howard Jones, "whether there was, according to the treaty of 1795, 'due and sufficient proof concerning the property thereof'; and, if so, whether the United States had the right to intervene in securing the property of the Spanish claimants."[10] Baldwin argued that the executive branch had overstepped its authority by seizing and imprisoning the captives, then again by acting as the agent of Ruiz and Montes, and later for the Spanish government as well. In addition to questioning the government's role as a party to the case, Baldwin also argued that Ruiz and Montes had falsified documents and therefore could not possibly claim the captives as slaves. Adams attacked the role of the executive, reminding the Supreme Court that the Van Buren administration had conspired at every turn to thwart the judicial process.[11] Although the Supreme Court justices believed that slavery was a matter of settled law in the United States, and although five of the nine justices on the Court were Southerners, the Court held in favor of the captives (with one dissent), following, in large measure, Baldwin's reasoning. If the captives were not legally slaves, and overwhelming evidence suggested that they were recently seized in Africa, they could not fall under the jurisdiction of Spanish law as property or as individuals liable for charges of murder and piracy. Since the cabin boy, Antonio, was clearly a slave under Spanish law, the Court ordered that he be returned to Cuba. The Court reversed, however, Judson's direction that the captives be returned to Africa at government expense, leaving the abolitionists the sizeable task of raising sufficient funds to send them home.[12] In the spring of 1841, the newly-freed *Amistad* Africans moved to Farmington, Connecticut, where they lived until November, when they sailed in the company of missionaries to Sierra Leone.[13]

Although the *Amistad* story was well known amongst scholars of abolition such as Bertram Wyatt-Brown and Benjamin Quarles and formed the basis for William Owens' *Slave Mutiny* (1953)—now in print under the title *Black Mutiny*—the production of *Amistad* by

Debbie Allen and Steven Spielberg reached a much broader audience when the film opened in December 1997. As Robert Brent Toplin observes, "Historical films help to shape the thinking of millions. Often the depictions on the screen influence the public's view much more than books do." The relationship between academic historians and their counterparts in film and fiction, however, has often been tempestuous. From the standpoint of many historians, historical films take unwarranted liberties with the sacred documentary record, imputing personal motivations to characters when they cannot be ascertained and adding fictitious persons and events to make the choppy record of the past appear seamless. Conversely, fans of historical film think that historians would impose the dreariness of the documentary form upon every decent story.[14] How, then, should historical films be judged? First, they must be judged based upon what they "say" rather than upon what the screenwriters, directors, and producers intend. Contrary to popular belief, a film can never be "just a movie." The themes and events developed on screen are filtered through the lens of prior knowledge and belief. In particular, the filmmakers' unquestioned assumptions can unwittingly reinforce the viewers' prejudices. Both Eric Foner and Leon Litwack, for example, criticized Ken Burn's monumental documentary, *The Civil War* (1990), on these grounds.[15]

In the crucial opening scenes of *Amistad*, Spielberg and David Franconi, the screenwriter, declare that the Africans themselves will be at the center of their historical narrative. Yet as the movie develops, it is equally apparent that they believe the *Amistad* story can also say something about the virtues of the American form of government. These two themes–African historical agency and the virtues of American democracy–are developed sequentially, so that the audience initially believes that the story is about the African captives but then realizes that there is a "greater" significance to the story. Howard Jones wrote that Spielberg "has . . . graphically depicted the 'middle passage' and other elements of nineteenth-century racial relations as a raw period in America's history that, like it or not, is an indelible part of our heritage. He has not made a black history movie; nor has he made a white history movie. He has made an American history movie that places the *Amistad* story within the nation's mainstream account of itself."[16] Certainly Allen, Spielberg, and Franconi brought to American audiences a story that, unlike the all-too-common paeans to the American past produced by Hollywood, challenged viewers to acknowledge the centrality of the horrific racism and genocide that was the Atlantic slave trade. Without ever depicting slavery in the United States, the film reminds viewers that this brutality was an integral part of American history. Historical authenticity mattered to the filmmakers, and numerous details in the film demonstrate a commitment to bring "history as it was" into the movie theaters. That said, the commitment to authenticity was limited. The trivial inaccuracies of the film—e.g., the freezing temperatures encountered by the captives when they arrived on Long Island *in late August*—do not matter. Even more substantial emendations, such as collapsing the original hearings and trials into one, have little effect on the overall story. At the other end of the spectrum, however, Spielberg manipulates the historical narrative to give the story meanings that it never had.

The difficulties begin immediately with the opening scenes onboard the *Amistad* as the captives free themselves, climb on deck, and kill five members of the crew. The documentary record shows that onboard the real *Amistad*, only the captain and the cook were killed for certain. The captives, Ruiz, and Montes confirmed this. Ruiz, Montes, and the cabin boy Antonio survived. The remaining two (not three) crew members may have been killed and thrown overboard, but they may also have jumped overboard in a vain attempt to swim to shore. In Hale Woodruff's 1939 painting, "The Mutiny" (which adorns the cover of Howard Jones' *Mutiny on the Amistad*), the two can be seen hastily lowering a boat in order to escape. More importantly, the gruesome death of the captain at Cinque's hands seems designed to provoke audience antipathy. Spielberg appears to defy viewers to judge the Africans harshly so that he can later, with the quite realistic scenes onboard the *Tecora*, enhance a feeling of sympathy and thereby justify Cinque's outrage. As Iyunolu Osagie observes, however, "The tie between blackness and violence in the movie reinforces rather than disentangles the mainstream American image of the black male body as violent."[17] This is especially the case because the film, which (erroneously) depicts the central legal issue as the Africans' origins, takes great pains to prove to the viewing audience that the captives are "really Africans." In contrast to Sean Wilentz's assertion in the *New Republic* that, "the filmmakers seem to have taken special care to make sure that the Africans acted authentically," observers should be wary about the ways in which the film encourages that belief. By acknowledging the differences among African peoples, and by using actors who could speak Mende, Spielberg goes farther than Hollywood has gone before. The authenticisms, by which I mean the cues provided to the audience to establish authenticity, are many. Aside from the Mende language, Spielberg brings us Africans who paddle a rowboat, are mystified by a bicycle, and "believe," as the character of John Quincy Adams intones, "that if one can summon the spirit of one's ancestors, then they have never left, and the wisdom and strengths they fathered will come to [their] aid." Only a specialist in African history (which I am not) could attest to the accuracy of these claims, but Osagie notes that a scene in which an angry Sengbe "takes off his clothes to dance away his frustrations" can only be understood "in light of Western expectations that an African dance around a fire is a necessary ingredient in the definition of Africanness."[18] In the search for African historical agency, the film's imagination derives from the filmmakers' presumptions.

Similarly the filmmakers stretch the *Amistad* tale into a morality play for American democracy. When reality didn't accord with the film's agenda, the past was made to suffer for it. The movie suggests that the central question at trial was the origin of the captives. It was not. Less than one month after the arrival of the *Amistad* in Connecticut, the U.S. district attorney said in open court, "I stand here. . . to contend that these blacks are freemen–that they have been brought within the jurisdiction of the United States, . . . and if found to be, as I suppose, native Africans, they may be sent to their native land." He even cited Joseph Story as the source of his conclusion that they should be returned to Africa.[19] The filmmakers also refused to embrace the seeming paradox of the real *Amistad* case, namely that a judge who had been instrumental in preventing Prudence Crandall from operating a school for black girls in Connecticut should be the one to order the captives freed and returned home. Instead, as the case appears to tip toward the Africans' side, they introduce a fictitious judge, a Van Buren appointee "monumentally insecure, particularly about his Roman Catholic heritage," who must weigh his conscience against political ambition. The real Judson, on the other hand, was an Andrew Jackson appointee to the federal bench and probably would, on many other issues, have sided with the Van Buren administration, but he did not. The depiction of Adams' legal arguments is preposterous. "How is it," the cinematic Adams inquires, "that a simple, plain property issue should find itself so ennobled as to be argued before the Supreme Court?" Adams didn't see the matter as a property rights case because it wasn't. In the film, Adams argues that the case concerns "the very nature of man" and claims that "the natural state of mankind—and I know this is a controversial idea—is freedom." Invoking the founding fathers as Sengbe invoked his ancestors, Adams convinces the Supreme Court that the Africans must be set free. By the end of the film, Adams sounds much more like an antislavery activist than he was in practice. This is rhetoric worthy of the American Anti-Slavery Society, whose Declaration of Sentiments in 1833 commented, "We have met together for the achievement of an enterprise, without which that of our fathers is incomplete, and which, for its magnitude, solemnity, and probable results upon the destiny of the world, as far transcends theirs as truth does to physical force." And elsewhere, "The right to enjoy liberty is inalienable."[20] As much as the filmmakers might wish that this were the essence of the case, the crucial issue in the *Amistad* case was whether or not an American court could look behind the *trespassos* to verify their authenticity. Contrary to the cinematic version, the American government actually argued in the Supreme Court that even if the captives were African, they should still be returned to Cuba.

To be sure, there were other distortions as well, changes which, although they may seem utterly innocuous, alter the historical narrative in subtle ways. The substitution of a British sea captain for Dr. Richard Madden, the British official who had resided in Cuba, at first seems harmless. The British captain authoritatively describes the horrors of the Middle Passage, providing information that nineteenth-century observers would have known well. The Atlantic slave trade to the United States, after all, had been banned for thirty years. Even the movie's most jarring scene, in which captives are thrown overboard from the *Tecora* in order to save on food supplies, parallels the well-known *Zong* massacre more than fifty years earlier.[21] In contrast, Madden impeached the *trespassos* carried by Ruiz and Montes, providing crucial evidence in the Africans' defense. Likewise, the appearance of the fictional Theodore Joadson, a former slave turned merchant in New England, demonstrates to the viewer that not all abolitionists were white. But Joadson is provided as a counter to Tappan, leading to an absurd conversation in which the fictional Tappan suggests that their cause might better be served if the captives became martyrs rather than free men and women. Moreover, Joadson, as the token black abolitionist in the film, is a poor substitute for the very real James W.C. Pennington of Hartford. Pennington was one of many black abolitionists who helped raise funds for the *Amistad* captives' defense and later stay in Farmington, Connecticut.[22]

The *Amistad* case provided abolitionists with an opportunity to unite around a common cause. While Tappan and his associates favored a gradual path toward abolition, they could unite with the immediate emancipationists in the Garrisonian wing of the movement because both agreed that the Africans' arrival in New England provided them with an unprecedented opportunity to strike at the legal underpinnings of slavery in America while freeing men, women, and children who were manifestly victims of the illegal African slave trade. Although the film laid great emphasis on communication difficulties, the outlines of the captives' story were apparent early on. To be sure, the abolitionists were not the only ones who wanted to shape public discourse surrounding the *Amistad* case. Even before the ship was captured off Long Island, newspaper accounts had been published describing, "A Spanish schooner sailed from Havana some six or eight weeks ago, with a number of slaves on board, and 26 white passengers, destined for St. Jago [Santiago] de Cuba. Intelligence was soon received that the blacks had risen upon the whites and put them to death, passengers, crew, and all."[23] Such obvious disinformation was clearly intended to evoke memories of slave rebellion in the American South: Nat Turner and his followers in Southampton County, Virginia, had murdered some 55 whites eight years earlier. From the beginning, Tappan and his associates knew that antislavery opponents would mold the story to suit their own political agenda. As the abolitionists sought to mold popular opinion, they sought to counter prevailing racist notions about Africans, emphasizing the humanity of Cinque, Grabeau, and the other captives. Consciously or unconsciously they also sought to distance themselves from the violence inherent in the shipboard uprising. Through their ambivalence toward violence, the antislavery activists obscured

African agency. Ironically, when the district court ruled in favor of the captives, Judson pronounced, "Cinque and Grabeau shall not sigh for Africa in vain. Bloody as may be their hands, they shall yet embrace their kindred." While the abolitionists shied away from the violence of the uprising, Judson's eloquent declaration defended insurrection in the face of tyranny. Not surprisingly, *The Charleston Mercury* ran the header, "The Pirate and Murderers Set Free!" and, quoting a New York paper, added "we find [Judson] writes much more like a heated partisan Abolitionist, than like a grave officer of justice."[24]

John Warner Barber's *History of the Amistad Captives*, published in May 1840, represents one important effort to mold popular opinion about the Africans and their case for freedom. Proceeding from one document to the next, the text weaves together legal proceedings, political documents, vignettes describing each African, and also "an article. . . giving an account of the efforts made for their intellectual and moral improvement, and some notice of the manners and customs prevalent in their native country."[25] The vignettes portray the captives as ordinary people with livelihoods and families torn apart by the international slave trade. Grabeau, "is married, but no children; he is a planter of rice." By his account, he was captured "on the road" and sold into slavery to pay a debt owed by his uncle. Bau had a wife and three children: "He was caught in the bush by 4 men as he was going to plant rice." Yaboi's "village was surrounded by soldiers, and he was taken by Gillewa, a Mendi man, to whom he was a slave ten years. Had a wife and one child. Gillewa sold him to Luiz, the Spaniard." Margru had "four sisters and two brothers; she was pawned by her father for a debt, which being unpaid, she was sold into slavery." Silhouettes depicting some of the captives were included, as was a phrenological examination of Cinque: "Firmness; self-esteem; hope–very large. Benevolence; veneration; conscientiousness; approbativeness; wonder; concentrativeness. . .–large," etc. Of course the conclusions drawn from phrenology were not science, but merely the reflection of the examiner's assumptions. Since Cinque's role in the shipboard uprising was well known even in the earliest weeks of the captives' stay in Connecticut, it is clear that the phrenologist described only as "Mr. Fletcher" supported the abolitionists' claim that the captives were not "pirates and murderers."[26]

In addition to providing descriptions of the captives' families and the circumstances surrounding their fate in the Atlantic slave trade, Barber used the text to authenticate the captives' stories and soften any aspects of those stories that might prejudice popular opinion. Tattooing, scarification, and other forms of body art were decidedly strange for those who had little contact with the maritime world. Konoma, for example, "is 5 ft. 4 in. in height, has large lips, and projecting mouth, his incisor teeth pressed outward and filed, giving him rather a savage appearance; he is the one who was supposed to be a cannibal, tattooed in the forehead with a diamond shaped figure." Elsewhere in his *History*, Barber acknowledges that the "papers designated one of the captives by the name of cannibal. The only reason for this appellation is, that his teeth, according to our notions, not being very well arranged, and a degree of emaciation leaving him but a skeleton, made him in fact a frightful object. Some of the front teeth of Konoma have been extracted, others have been sharpened, and made to project from his mouth like tusks." When asked why he desired this appearance, he replied, "to make the ladies love him." And then, just to make sure that he drove his point home, Barber added, "that the captives without distinction appear filled with horror at the idea of feasting upon human flesh."[27] Where Mende and other West African customs appeared strange, Barber hastened to place them in familiar terms. He softened polygamy by describing courtship in romantic terms, yet hastened to assure his readers that women were still subordinate to men even in death. He encouraged onlookers shocked by the expressive "weeping and mourning" of the captives' funerals (apparent because several died in Connecticut) to imagine that "the stillness attending exercises of this kind among us seems surprising, and to be accounted for only on the ground of insensibility." Even though the African origins of the captives were acknowledged early in the case, Barber endeavored to prove to his readers that the captives were indeed of African origin and had suffered the injustices they described. He noted that Konoma "recognizes many words in Mungo Park's Mandingo vocabulary" and that the village Bar-tu claimed as his home really did exist as it had been "visited by Major Laing." P-ie "recognizes with great readiness the Timmani words and phrases contained in Winterbottom's account of Sierra Leone."[28] Barber, incidentally, did not seem to be aware of the condescension inherent in suggesting that the captives were really Africans because they can recognize the faint glimmers of their own world through the imperial eyes of Europeans.

If the antislavery activists were themselves anxious to mold popular discourse about the *Amistad* captives, how might an Atlantic World perspective enrich the popular and historical understanding of the *Amistad*? Four dimensions of the *Amistad* story require further attention: 1) the context of the Atlantic slave trade and the Middle Passage; 2) the role of slavery in nineteenth-century plantation economies; 3) race and the character of Northern abolition; and, 4) the role of admiralty law in the *Amistad* verdict. Much like the abolitionists, the fictional accounts have difficulty acknowledging the historical agency of the captives. Clearly within the context of the Atlantic slave trade, and the Middle Passage in particular, that autonomy was heavily constrained. Abolitionists sought to portray the captives as largely helpless victims of the slave trade. At the same time, they were anxious to limit any possible criticism of the captives themselves. Two examples will serve to illustrate why the question of agency is so terribly vexed. During the district court trial, Holabird introduced evidence that suggested that Cinque had owed a debt and sold two people into slavery to cover that debt. When one ran away, Cinque himself was seized by his creditor in payment. The captives' counsel successfully convinced the court that this evidence was mistaken.[29] In 1953, William Owens wrote in *Slave Mutiny* that Cinque returned to Africa only to become a slave trader himself. Howard Jones has demonstrated how this fictional rendition was in turn taken as fact by a number of historians, including Samuel Elliott Morison, C. Vann Woodward, Bertram Wyatt-Brown, and Paul Finkelman.[30] Barring a dramatic discovery, no evidence will ever reveal much more about the captives' lives either before their capture or after their return. The accounts they provided while in the United States, plus the fragmentary clues in the American Missionary Association's archives, are the only written records available to scholars. While the accusation that Cinque took advantage of the antislavery activists' efforts to enrich himself in the slave trade is clearly pernicious, the entanglement in West African forms of servitude is not. John Barber's *History of the Amistad Captives* clearly shows that, for example, Shule and Faginna were sentenced to enslavement as judicial punishments.

Kagne, Margru, and Grabeau were sold into slavery to pay off debts. Yet, west African forms of servitude were not the equivalent of slavery.[31]

Equally problematic is the rationale provided by the captives' attorneys for the shipboard uprising, namely that the cook had intimated that the captives would be eaten. An account by Grabeau provided to the abolitionists for publication on October 7 confirms this story. Can this story be taken at face value? All of the literary versions accept the story as fact.[32] Understood in context, the claim that the captives feared white cannibalism strains credulity. Are we to believe that Africans enslaved in the late 1830s were unaware of the plantation labor that awaited them across the Atlantic? And even if they were, does it not seem likely given the number of African people within the Atlantic maritime world, or in the barracoons of Havana, that this ignorance would be dispelled before they rose up against the captain and crew of the *Amistad*? Antislavery activists repudiated violence, Quakers as a matter of religious principle, but others more generally because they could not bring themselves to advocate slave uprisings. Self-defense, as the celebration of abolitionist Elijah Lovejoy's martyrdom suggests, was another matter.[33] Intriguingly, *The Interesting Narrative of the Life of Olaudah Equiano*, originally published in 1789, contains a similar story with which abolitionists would have been familiar. When Equiano first saw the Atlantic slaver that would carry him to sea, he asked other Africans "if we were not to be eaten by those white men with horrible looks, red faces, and long hair." After they arrived in Barbados, "old slaves" told Equiano and his companions that they "were not to be eaten." Either the fear of cannibalism was endemic to the West African coast (encompassing both Mende and Igbo peoples) or the story was planted ex post facto by abolitionists anxious to distance themselves from the advocacy of violence.[34]

Easily overlooked in the drama of the *Amistad* story is the place of that tale within the larger history of slavery and racism in the Atlantic World. Both the Cuban plantations that the African captives escaped, as well as the Connecticut shores upon which they found themselves, had a far more complex historical position than any popular rendition could suggest. While New England was the home of abolitionist sentiment in the United States, Cuba was, in 1839, still a growing plantation economy, dependent upon the importation of enslaved Africans for sugar production. Ironically the success of the Haitian Revolution (1798-1804) provided the economic foundations for the primacy of sugar cultivation in Cuba. According to Franklin Knight, despite the abolition of the British slave trade in 1807, and an Anglo-Spanish treaty in 1817 that legally ended the Spanish slave trade, Cuban slave traders and planters imported approximately 387,000 enslaved Africans between 1835 and 1864. Between 1824 and 1866, British naval vessels stationed off the coast of Cuba had intercepted more than 26,000 African captives. Theoretically, such captives became *emancipados* (freedmen) but in practice the right to their labor was sold as if they were slaves.[35] But in one important respect, Cuban plantation slavery must have stood out in the minds of American abolitionists. In Cuba, the plantation economy had grown almost entirely in the nineteenth century. There were African slaves before 1800 to be sure, just as there were increasing numbers of Chinese contract workers after 1847, but from the standpoint of Northern abolitionists, the Cuban plantation economy proved that the slave trade and slavery were not moribund institutions in the Atlantic World.

New England and neighboring New York were also part of the Atlantic World. Textile factories and clothing manufacturers in the North depended upon supplies of Southern cotton. The hypocrisy of challenging slavery in the South while purchasing goods produced by slaves was so clear that a "free produce" movement flourished amongst antislavery activists. For example, black abolitionists at the 1836 convention of the American Moral Reform Society challenged "Colored Churches in the Free States" to acknowledge that, "the criminality attendant on the existence of American slavery is national—and that all who aid or abet this 'accursed traffic' in the *bodies* and *souls* of men, by purchase, sale, or barter, in either their persons, or the products thereof—are guilty of producing all the rapine, blood, murder, and cruelties, in which the system itself so much abounds."[36] The Atlantic maritime world was interconnected. The fictional accounts also suggest that the presence of African peoples in the North was somehow strange, and yet Jeffrey Bolster estimates that one-fifth of all American sailors were black. They were highly visible and active members of maritime communities from Charleston through Baltimore, New York, and Boston. David Walker's *Appeal to the Coloured Citizens of the*

World (1829) was carried from Boston into the South by black mariners and may well have been familiar to Nat Turner in Virginia.[37] While black abolitionism flourished throughout the North, a fact overlooked in the fictional accounts, it was especially active in maritime communities like New Bedford, Massachusetts. Indeed, it should be no surprise that given the interconnectedness of the Atlantic World, the captive Burnah spoke some English, while Lieutenant Meade, "who speaks Spanish both elegantly and fluently acted as an interpreter between the Spaniards and the court" during the initial inquiry onboard the *Washington*.[38]

Finally, Don Fehrenbacher suggested that the Van Buren administration was prepared to turn the *Amistad* captives over to Spain, but it did not reckon with the independence of the federal judiciary. It should be added that it did not reckon with the independence of the nation's own naval officers who sought salvage rights to the *Amistad*, its cargo and alleged slaves, thus triggering the legal chain of events that brought the case to the Supreme Court. Before Justice Story could order the *Amistad* captives free according to the "eternal principles of justice," he had to deal with the questions of admiralty law that were central to the case. Under the federal Judiciary Act of 1789, federal district courts gained the responsibility of hearing admiralty cases. Thus Judge Andrew Judson held the initial hearing on board the *Washington*, and it was to his district court that Lieutenants Meade and Gedney filed their libel for salvage. Nor is it surprising that Justice Joseph Story was chosen to write the decision. He was an eminent jurist, after all, whose *Commentaries on the Constitution* (1833) covered admiralty proceedings in some detail.[39] In his decision, Story argued that the central claims made by the United States government were those pertaining to the ninth article of the Treaty of 1819 which read, "that all ships and merchandize, of what nature so ever, which shall be rescued out of the hands of any pirates or robbers, on the high seas, shall be brought into some port of either states, and shall be delivered to the custody of the officers of that port, in order to be taken care of and restored, entire, to the true proprietor, as soon as due and sufficient proof shall be made concerning the property thereof."

"To bring the case within the article," Story continued, "it is essential to establish: 1st, That these negroes, under all the circumstances, fall within the description of merchandize, in the sense of the treaty: 2d, That there has been a rescue of them on the high seas, out of the hands of pirates and robbers; which, in the present case, can only be, by showing that they themselves are pirates and robbers: and 3d, That Ruiz and Montez, the asserted proprietors, are the proprietors, and have established their title by competent proof."[40] Had the men and women on the *Amistad* been slaves, the court saw "no reason why they may not justly be deemed. . . merchandize." And yet clearly they were not, for District Attorney Holabird had acknowledged that they were taken from Africa. To the claim that the American government had no power to look behind the documentary facade, Story replied that such documents "are always open to be impugned for fraud; and whether that fraud be in the original obtaining of these documents, or in the subsequent fraudulent and illegal use of them, when once it is satisfactorily established, it overthrows all their sanctity, and destroys them as proof." The court was not, he maintained, threatening the "intercourse of nations" in so doing. Quite the contrary, it was an "every day's occurrence" in admiralty proceedings. When a vessel claims "privileges, immunities, or rights," for example, under a false flag, it is "the duty of our courts to strip off the disguise, and to look at the case, according to its naked realities."[41]

Seen within the Atlantic World context, the story of the *Amistad* and the Africans who escaped the bonds of slavery is both less and more significant than fictional accounts have acknowledged. By distinguishing between the legal reasoning of the Supreme Court decision and the peripheral language used to support it, it is apparent that the scope of the decision was extremely narrow. Neither the language nor the result of the decision presaged any change in the status of African peoples in the United States. If anything, as Howard Jones suggests, it may have reinforced in Chief Justice Roger Brooke Taney's mind the arguments that he later made in the Dred Scott case. Confiding in his diary before his Supreme Court appearance, Adams wrote that he prepared "with deep anguish of heart, and painful search of means to defeat and expose the abominable conspiracy, Executive and Judicial, of this Government, against the lives of those wretched men."[42] In this both he and Baldwin succeeded, but only because they made the *Amistad* captives' story fit within American legal discourse. So, too, did the abolitionists shape the discourse around the *Amistad* captives, blurring their historical agency in the re-telling of the tale. The real victory belonged to the captives themselves. At the same time, the *Amistad*'s voyage brought together pieces of the Atlantic World accustomed to seeing themselves as separate. It brought the mentality of the aggressively capitalistic sugar plantation economy in Cuba into contact with an equally capitalistic American North that saw slavery as incompatible with progress. All of the parties to the *Amistad* uprising and their historians might well understand Inga Clendinnen's observation based upon her research on Spaniards and Maya in sixteenth-century Yucatan: "In the course of that struggle about the nature of the alien and other, they were sometimes forced to unsought and profoundly disquieting discoveries about themselves–which is always a danger in the hall-of-mirrors world we make when we seek to possess the strange and make it part of ourselves."[43]

Notes

Morrison

1 Samuel Shaw, *The Journals of Major Samuel Shaw, the First American Consul at Canton*, Josiah Quincy, ed. (Taipei: Ch'end-Wen, 1968), 234.

2 Ibid., 183.

3 Fisher Ames, eulogy on George Washington, 8 February 1800, cited in Merry Weisner, *Discovering the Global Past* (Boston: Houghton Mifflin, 1997), 204.

4 Benjamin Labaree, et al., *America and the Sea: A Maritime History* (Mystic, Connecticut: Mystic Seaport, 1998), 259.

5 Cited in Ralph D. Paine, *The Ships and Sailors of Old Salem: The Record of a Brilliant Era of American Achievement* (Boston: Charles E. Lauriat, 1924), 147.

6 [Goberdhan] Bhagat, "America's First Contacts with India, 1784-1785," *The American Neptune* (January 1971): 39; Dorothy Schurman Hawes, "To the Farthest Gulf. Outline of the Old China Trade," *Essex Institute Historical Collections* 77, 2 (April 1941): 117.

7 Hawes, "To the Farthest Gulf," 130.

8 Ibid., 132.

9 Ibid., 112, 141.

10 *New Hampshire Gazette*, January 9, 1790.

11 Michael Warner, *The Letters of the Republic: Publication and the Public Sphere in Eighteenth-Century America* (Cambridge, Massachusetts: Harvard University Press, 1990), Chap. 5 passim.

12 Drew R. McCoy, *The Elusive Republic: Political Economy in Jeffersonian America* (Chapel Hill: University of North Carolina Press, 1980), 20.

13 Ibid., 57, 60, 187.

14 Ibid., 168.

15 Richard L. Bushman, *The Refinement of America: Persons, Houses, Cities* (New York: Vintage, 1993), 28.

16 Ibid., 33.

17 Shaw, *Journals*, Appendix 43.

18 Ibid., 181.

19 Hawes, "To the Farthest Gulf," 121.

20 Amasa Delano, *Delano's Voyages of Commerce and Discovery: Amasa Delano in China, the Pacific Islands, Australia, and South America,* 1789-1807, Eleanor Roosevelt Seagram, ed. (Stockbridge, Massachusetts: Berkshire House, 1994), 368.

21 Edmund Fanning, *Voyages and Discoveries in the South Seas, 1792-1832* (1833; New York: Dover, 1989), 188-89.

22 Shaw, *Journals,* 180-81.

23 Ibid., 181.

24 Ibid., 317.

25 James Duncan Phillips, *Pepper and Pirates: Adventures in the Sumatra Pepper Trade of Salem* (Cambridge, Massachusetts: The Riverside Press, 1949), 74.

26 Also spelled *fan kwei.*

27 C. Toogood Downing, *The Fan-Qui in China in 1636-1637,* 3 vols. (1838; New York: Barnes & Noble, 1972), 1:v. Downing goes on to explain, "the term of reproach, therefore, if such it still be, expresses in China, not only the English, but all Europeans, Americans, Parsees, Arabs, Malays, and the inhabitants of every other quarter of the globe, excepting their own Celestial Empire" (1:v-vi.). Although in time Americans came to have more appreciation for the rest of Downings's sentence–"but having been so long accustomed to the epithet, and hearing it so often pro-nounced, we are willing to hope that it is now generally used without intention to insult, and may be fairly translated 'Foreigner,'"–in the early days of their involvement in the China Trade, they were more sensitive to the original meaning of the term.

28 Robert L. Peabody, *The Log of the Grand Turks* (New York: Houghton Mifflin, 1926), 79; Hawes, "To the Farthest Gulf," 122.

29 Jacques M. Downs, *The Golden Ghetto: The American Commercial Community at Canton and the Shaping of American China Policy, 1784-*

1844 (Bethlehem, Pennsylvania: Lehigh University Press, 1997), 39, 73; Hawes, "To the Farthest Gulf," 110.

30 Peabody, *Grand Turks*, 79.

31 Downs, *Golden Ghetto*, 61.

32 Shaw, *Journals*, 178-79.

33 Robert Bennet Forbes to Rose Forbes, April 14, 1839, cited in Robert Bennet Forbes, *Letters from China: The Canton-Boston Correspondence of Robert Bennet Forbes, 1838-1840*, Phyllis Forbes Kerr, ed. (Mystic, Connecticut: Mystic Seaport, 1996), 118.

34 Ezra Stiles, *The United States Elevated to Glory and Honor*, cited in McCoy, *Elusive Republic*, 89.

35 John Warren, "An Oration Delivered July 4, 1783," cited in McCoy, *Elusive Republic*, 89. See also C. Toogood Downing's extollation of commerce noted in his 1839 reflections on two decades in Canton: "Commerce herself must rejoice to see so many of her votaries collected together, and must feel proud of their station and importance, and that it is through her means that nations are enabled to send so large a fleet yearly to China, and to return almost wholly laden with one single article of luxury" (Downing, *Fan-Qui*, 1:79).

36 Cited in Labaree, *America and the Sea*, 239-40.

37 Downing, *Fan-Qui*, 39.

38 Downs, *The Golden Ghetto*, 73; Hawes, "To the Farthest Gulf," 111.

39 Downs, *The Golden Ghetto*, 73-74.

40 Shaw, *Journals*, 184.

41 Fanning, *Voyages and Discovery*, 183.

42 Ibid., 184.

43 Ibid., 183.

44 Ibid., 189.

45 Ibid., 225.

46 Downing, *Fan-Qui*, 1:2-3.

47 Shaw, *Journals*, 183.

48 William C. Hunter, *Bits of Old China* (1855; Taipei: Ch'eng-Wen, 1966), 4.

49 Walter Muir Whitehill, ed., "Remarks on the Canton Trade and the Manner of Transacting Business," *Essex Institute Historical Collections* 73, 4 (October 1937): 307.

50 Ibid., 305.

51 Ibid., 307.

52 Ibid., 306.

53 McCoy, *Elusive Republic*, 87.

54 Fanning, *Voyages and Discoveries*, 184.

55 Ibid., 186.

56 Ibid., 184.

57 Downs, *Golden Ghetto*, 61.

58 Ibid., 61.

59 Ibid.

60 Ibid.

61 Shaw, *Journals*, 61.

62 Ibid., 185.

63 Ibid., 186.

64 Ibid.

65 Ibid., 181.

66 Ibid., 235.

67 Fanning, *Voyages and Discoveries*, 225.

68 Ibid, 187.

69 Ibid.

70 Shaw, *Journals*, 190-91.

71 Downing, *Fan-Qui*, 1:62-63.

72 Shaw, *Journals*, 227-28.

73 Cited in McCoy, *Elusive Republic*, 90.

74 Downing, *Fan-Qui*, 1:2, 33, 39; Fanning, *Voyages and Discoveries*, 40, 184.

75 Archibald Robbins, *A Journal, Comprising an Account of the Loss of the Brig Commerce…*, 1831, cited in Paul Baepler, *White Slaves, African Masters: An Anthology of American Barbary Captivity Narratives* (Chicago, University of Chicago Press, 1999), 33.

Shannon

1 Ian Robertson, *Sociology*, 3rd ed. New York: Worth Publishers, Inc., 1993), 132.

2 Glen H. Elder Jr., Eliza K. Pavalko, and Elizabeth C. Clipp, *Working with Archival Data: Studying Lives* (Thousand Oaks, California: Sage Publications, California: 1993), 7. See also: Glen H. Elder Jr., John Modell, and Ross D. Parke, *Children in Time and Place: Developmental and Historical Insights.* (Cambridge and New York: Cambridge University Press, 1993), 11.

3 Elder et al., *Children in Time and Place*, 11.

4 Ibid.

5 Ibid.

6 Elizabeth Forman Crane, ed., *The Diary of Elizabeth Drinker.* (Boston, Massachusetts: Northeastern University Press, 1991). Born in 1735, Elizabeth Sandwich Drinker began keeping a diary at the age of 23. The Crane edition of the diary fills three volumes and includes accounts of such events as the British occupation of Philadelphia and the yellow fever epidemic of 1793.

7 Ibid., 786.

8 From her writings we know of other children–black, white, and Indian– who were present in the Drinker house as servants.

9 The three black children referred to are Peter Savage, Scipio Drake, and Peter Woodward.

10 Alice Wright was a nurse paid by the Drinkers. She often recommended black people to the Drinkers, and her endorsement seemed to hold merit. Moreover, Alice apparently employed servants herself. When the ship *Ganges* arrived in Philadelphia, she told Elizabeth that "she wants one of the blacks that are still down the river, to be bound to her…." Alice died on February 25, 1803. Elizabeth offered a "Windingsheet and other things to bury her in." She was buried on February 26, 1803, at the Methodists Ground. Peter Woodward attended the funeral; Elizabeth did not (Crane, *Diary of Elizabeth Drinker*, 1329, 1630).

11 One of Philadelphia's leading residents, Benjamin Rush was a physician, abolitionist, and member of the board of the House of Employment.

12 Ibid., 786.

13 The Acting Committee of Pennsylvania Abolition Society (PAS), the Committee of Guardians, the Philadelphia House of Employment, and Overseers of the Poor.

14 Thomas M. Doerflinger. *A Vigorous Spirit of Enterprise* (Chapel Hill: University of North Carolina Press, 1986).

15 Michael Grossberg. *Governing the Hearth: Law and the Family in Nineteenth Century America* (Chapel Hill: University of North Carolina Press, 1985), 19.

16 Gary B. Nash and Jean R. Soderlund. *Freedom by Degrees: Emancipation in Pennsylvania and Its Aftermath* (New York: Oxford University Press, 1991).

17 This indenture period (until the age of 21) distinguished free-born children from others whose mothers were enslaved at the time they were born. For the latter, the period of indenture lasted until they were 28 years of age.

18 A hostler was one who took care of the horses; a groom.

19 Scipio Drake, one of the three black children present at the Drinker home when Peter arrived, could not be disciplined and was sent to live at another place. Prior to coming to the Drinker home he had been in jail for running away from where he had been placed.

20 Crane, *Diary of Elizabeth Drinker*, 1991.

21 Ibid.

22 Ibid.

23 Ibid., 1879.

24 W. Jeffrey Bolster, "'To Feel Like a Man': Black Seamen in the Northern States, 1800-1860." *Journal of American History* (March, 1990): 1182.

25 Between 1794 and 1822 the number of ships leaving Philadelphia for Cuba increased by "four percent per year." And, although there was a slight decline in sailings from 1802 to 1803, after that brief period sailings from Philadelphia to Cuba increased dramatically, reaching an all-time peak in 1806 and 1807. Linda K. Salvucci, "Supply, Demand, and the Making of a Market: Philadelphia and Havana at the Beginning of the Nineteenth Century," in Franklin W. Knight and Peggy K. Liss, eds.

Atlantic Port Cities: Economy, Culture and Society in the Atlantic World,
1650-1850 (Knoxville: University of Tennessee Press, 1991), 41.

26 The protection certificate was an official document that described the
   seaman and attested to his legal status. In spite of this documentation, a
   number of black men were kidnapped and sold into slavery.

27 Crane, *Diary of Elizabeth Drinker*, 1991.

28 Ibid,. 1879.

29 A person on a merchant ship in charge of the commercial activities of
   the vessel.

30 Martha S. Putney. *Black Sailors.* New York: Greenwood Press, 1987, 12.

31 Crane, *Diary of Elizabeth Drinker*, 1903.

32 Ibid., 1904.

33 John Moffet, age 19, from Philadelphia; George Shewell, age 20, from
   Philadelphia; John Roberts, age not listed, a native of New York; Thomas
   Roberts, age 28, a native of New York; and John Low, age 22, from
   Boston. Crew Lists, Historical Society of Pennsylvania, 29.

34 Seamen's Protection Certificate issued to Peter Woodward.

35 The Lazaretto refers to the Pest House erected on Fisher's Island, later
   known as Province Island, "purchased and owned by the Province, for
   the use of sick persons arriving from sea," John F. Watson, *Annals of
   Philadelphia and Pennsylvania* (Philadelphia, Pennsylvania, 1845), 461.

36 Crane, *Diary of Elizabeth Drinker*, 1991.

37 John Moore, also known as Sam Moore, was indentured to Jacob
   Downing, the Drinkers' son-in-law, on December 6, 1802, for a period of
   five years (PAS Indenture Book D, 76).

38 Crane, *Diary of Elizabeth Drinker*, 1991.

39 Emanuel Eyres, also known as Manuel Eyres, was a shipwright and a
   Presbyterian whose household in Northern Liberties in 1790 was com-
   prised of two free white males over the age of sixteen, three free white
   males under the age of 15, eight free white females, one other free person, and four slaves, Crane; *Heads of Families at the First Census of the
   United States, 1790. Pennsylvania* (Washington, D.C.: U.S. Government
   Printing Office, 1907), 204.

40 Crane, *Diary of Elizabeth Drinker*, 1991.

41 Ibid., 2015.

42 Ibid., 2091.

43 In 1773, Atsion Forge in New Jersey was sold to Henry Drinker, Abel James, and Lawrence Saltar. The partners formed and operated the Atsion Company. Years later a rift developed, and in 1805 the property was sold. The purchasers were the same Henry Drinker and Jacob Downing, his son-in-law. The ironworks was a prosperous venture for the owners for many years. Finally, in 1822, as a result of foreclosure, the property was sold to Samuel Richards, Arthur D. Pierce, *Iron in the Pines* (New Brunswick: New Jersey: Rutgers University Press, 1957).

44 Crane, *Diary of Elizabeth Drinker*, 1991.

45 Ibid.

46 Salvucci, Linda K., "Supply, Demand and the Making of a Market," 42-43.

Winch

1 On the visit of Forten and Dunbar to Alderman Tod, see Seamen's Protection Certificates, 1810, Port of Philadelphia, National Archives.

2 For an account of the remarkable career of James Forten, see Julie Winch, *A Gentleman of Color: The Life of James Forten* (New York: Oxford University Press, 2002).

3 Winch, *A Gentleman of Color*, 63-65, 74-76, 84-89.

4 Ibid., 8-23.

5 Ibid., 23-52.

6 For an overview of African American community life in Philadelphia in the late eighteenth and early nineteenth centuries, see Julie Winch, ed., *The Elite of Our People: Joseph Willson's Sketches of Black Upper-Class Life in Antebellum Philadelphia* (University Park: Penn State University Press, 2000), 1-50.

7 St. Paul's Church, Philadelphia, Baptisms, 1782-1828; Marriages, 1759-1829; Burials, 1790-1852, 292, Historical Society of Pennsylvania (hereafter cited as HSP).

8 Robert Purvis, *Remarks on the Life and Character of James Forten, Delivered at Bethel Church, March 30, 1842* (Philadelphia: Merrihew and Thompson, 1842), 8.

9 For the birthdates of the four Dunbar children see (Old Swedes) Gloria Dei–Marriages, 1795-1816, 2133, HSP; Seamen's Protection Certificates for the Port of Philadelphia (1810), National Archives; Philadelphia Crew Lists, 1813, 37, HSP; Parish Register of St. Thomas's African Episcopal Church, Philadelphia, Archives of St. Thomas's Church (courtesy of the minister, vestry, and members of the church).

10 Philadelphia city directories, 1792, 1798, 1799; Winch, *A Gentleman of Color*, 77-87, 101-102.

11 *Poulson's American Daily Advertiser*, April 10, 1805.

12 (Old Swedes) Gloria Dei–Marriages, 1795-1816, 2133; U.S. census, 1810: Philadelphia, Cedar Ward, 255; Philadelphia city directories, 1811, 1816, 1817.

13 Philadelphia city directories, 1811, 1813, 1814; U.S. census, 1810: Philadelphia County, Moyamensing, 129; Seamen's Protection Certificates, Port of Philadelphia (1810); Philadelphia Crew Lists, 1810, 75; 1815, 102; 1816, 113.

14 Philadelphia Crew Lists, 1813, 37; 1817, 187, 344; Philadelphia city directory, 1824.

15 Donald R. Hickey, *The War of 1812: A Forgotten Conflict* (Urbana: University of Illinois Press, 1990), 11; James Forten was well aware of the vulnerability of African American sailors. See Winch, *A Gentleman of Color*, 86-87.

16 Seamen's Protection Certificates, Port of Philadelphia (1810).

17 Philadelphia Crew Lists, 1819, 123.

18 W. Jeffrey Bolster, *Black Jacks: African American Seamen in the Age of Sail* (Cambridge, Massachusetts: Harvard University Press, 1997), 236.

19 Philadelphia Crew Lists, 1821, 27.

20 Bolster, *Black Jacks*, 191-209.

21 Christ Church; Marriages, Confirmations and Communicants, 1800-1900, 4787, HSP.

22 Philadelphia Crew Lists, 1823, 163, 226; 1825A, 122; 1826A, 59.

23 Ibid., 1828, 118; 1838, 298. Philadelphia city directories, 1825, 1829, 1830, 1833. U.S. census, 1830: Philadelphia, Pine Ward, 338.

24 Philadelphia Board of Health Records, HSP.

25 *Keys to Enlistment,* vol. 2 (Boston, October 28, 1846), National Archives.

26 Ibid. (Boston, September 28, 1848).

27 Ibid. (New York, February 3, 1851). Rendezvous Reports, 1854 (New York, February 1854); 1855, 222. Record Group 24, National Archives.

28 Rendezvous Reports, 1858, 33; 1859, 6.

29 Ibid., 1861, 60; 1862, 73.

30 Ibid. 1863, 306; 1863, 306, 363. Because Dunbar enlisted in Boston, rather than his native Pennsylvania, his service was credited to Massachusetts. See *Massachusetts Soldiers, Sailors, and Marines in the Civil War* (Norwood, Massachusetts, 1933), vol. 7, 851. The literature on the role of black sailors in the United States Navy during the Civil War is very limited. Happily, a recent work, Steven J. Ramold's *Slaves, Sailors, Citizens: African Americans in the Union Navy* (Dekalb: Northern Illinois University Press, 2002), sheds light on the experience not only of ex-slaves but on the likes of James Forten Dunbar, freeborn men of color who volunteered for service.

31 Rendezvous Records, 1863, 363. For a discussion of the significance of sailors' tattoos, see Simon P. Newman, "Reading the Bodies of Early American Seafarers," *William and Mary Quarterly* 55 (January 1998): 63, 69-70, 72, 79.

32 Register of Admissions to United States Naval Asylum, Philadelphia, Pennsylvania, 1865-85; Record Group 52, Records of the Bureau of Medicine and Surgery, Department of the Navy; Monthly Muster Roll of Pensioners and Beneficiaries of the United States Naval Asylum, Philadelphia, Pennsylvania, for the month ending the 31st day of January 1870, Record Group 71, Records of the Bureau of Docks and Yards, Department of the Navy, National Archives, Mid-Atlantic Region, Philadelphia.

33 On the political career of William Deas Forten, see Winch, *A Gentleman of Color,* 367-71.

34 Records of United States Naval Asylum—Monthly Reports of Admissions, Deaths and Changes (1865-88), Record Group 181, Records of Naval Districts and Shore Establishments, Department of the Navy, National Archives, Mid-Atlantic Region.

1 Louis Armstrong, *Satchmo: My Life in New Orleans* (New York: Prentice Hall, 1954); *Swing That Music* (New York: Da Capo, 1993); Richard Meryman, *Louis Armstrong: A Self-Portrait* (New York: Eakins Press, 1971).

2 James Clifford, *Routes: Travel and Translation in the Late Twentieth Century* (Cambridge, Massachusetts: Harvard University Press, 1997).

3 Interview with Captain William F. Carroll, son-in-law of Joseph Streckfus, St. Louis, Missouri, January 20, 2000; Delores Jane Meyer, "Excursion Steamboating on the Mississippi with Streckfus Steamers, Inc." (Ph.D diss., St. Louis University, 1967).

4 *St. Louis Argus*, July 27, 1921, 5.

5 George Foster with Tom Stoddard, *Pops Foster: The Autobiography of a New Orleans Jazzman* (Berkeley: University of California Press, 1971), 110-11.

6 Miles Davis, who was raised in East St. Louis, Illinois, used this label to describe the music of the Mississippi Valley region around St. Louis. Miles Davis with Quincy Troupe, *Miles: the Autobiography* (New York: Simon & Schuster, 1990), 42.

7 W.T. Lhamon Jr., *Raising Cain: Blackface Performance from Jim Crow to Hip Hop* (Cambridge: Harvard University Press, 1998), ch. 2.

8 Joe William Trotter Jr., *River Jordan: African American Urban Life in the Ohio Valley* (Lexington: University of Kentucky Press, 1998); *Cincinnati Union*, July 8, 1920, 1; Lyle Koehler, *Cincinnati's Black Peoples: A Chronology and Bibliography, 1787-1982* (Cincinnati: Neighborhood & Community Studies, 1986).

9 Nicholas Lemann, *The Promised Land: The Great Black Migration and How It Changed America* (New York: Vintage Books, 1992), describes the "mix of optimism and disgust" felt by migrants in the Mississippi Delta.

10 *St. Louis Argus*, May 14, 1926, 3.

11 *Life on the Mississippi* in *Mississippi Writings* (New York: Library of America, 1982), 217-616. Among the influential fictional explorations of the riverboats are Frances Parkinson Keyes, *Steamboat Gothic* (New York: Julian Messner, 1952) and Edna Ferber, *Show Boat* (Garden City, New York: Doubleday, Page, 1926).

12 George F. Roth Jr., "Those Elegant Enjoyments," in Joyce V.B. Cauffield & Carolyn E. Banfield, eds., *The River Book: Cincinnati and the Ohio* (Cincinnati, Ohio: The Program for Cincinnati, 1981), 52-59.

13 Mary Wheeler, *Steamboatin' Days: Folk Songs of the River Packet Era* (Baton Rouge: Louisiana State University Press, 1944).

14 *St. Louis Argus*, July 27, 1921, 5.

15 Gaston Bachelard, *"Water and Dreams"*: An Annotated Translation with Introduction by the Translator, Edith Rodgers Farrell, trans. (Ph.D diss., University of Iowa, 1965).

16 Teagarden, as quoted in Laurence Bergreen, *Louis Armstrong: An Extravagant Life* (New York: Broadway Books, 1997), 148.

17 John Urry, *The Tourist Gaze: Leisure and Travel in Contemporary Societies* (London: Sage Publications, 1990), 10.

Trivelli & Williams

1 See Paul Gilroy, *The Black Atlantic: Modernity and Double Consciousness* (Cambridge, Massachusetts: Harvard University Press, 1993); Ira Berlin, "From Creole to African: Atlantic Creoles and the Origins of African American Society in Mainland North America," *William and Mary Quarterly* 53, 2 (April 1996): 251-89; and Dwayne E. Williams, "Rethinking the African Diaspora: A Comparative Look at Race and Identity in a Transatlantic Community, 1878-1921," in Darlene Clark Hine and Jacqueline McLeod, eds, *Crossing Boundaries: Comparative History of Black People*, (Bloomington: Indiana University Press, 1999), 105-20.

2 See W. Jeffery Bolster, *Black Jacks: African American Seamen in the Age of Sail* (Cambridge, Massachusetts: Harvard University Press, 1997); Martha S. Putney, *Black Sailors: Afro-American Merchant Seamen and Whalemen Prior to the Civil War* (Westport, Connecticut: Greenwood Press, 1987); Lamont D. Thomas, *Paul Cuffe: Black Entrepreneur and Pan-Africanist* (Urbana: University of Illinois Press, 1986); Peter Linebaugh and Marcus Rediker, *The Many-Headed Hydra: Sailors, Slaves, Commoners, and the Hidden History of the Revolutionary Atlantic* (Boston, Massachusetts: Beacon Press, 2000); Julie Winch, *A Gentleman of Color: The Life of James Forten* (Oxford: Oxford University Press, 2002).

3 The authors acknowledge Dr. Robert A. Hill, editor of the *Marcus Garvey and Universal Negro Improvement Association Papers*, for his encourage-

ment. Their research was funded by the Paul Cuffe Fellowship for the Study of Minorities in American Maritime History.

4 According to the preamble of the UNIA constitution, the group was a "society ... working for the general uplift of the Negro peoples of the world." Robert A. Hill, ed. *The Marcus Garvey and Universal Negro Improvement Association Papers* (Berkeley, California: University of California Press, 1983), 1:256 (hereafter cited as "Hill, *Garvey Papers*").

5 Joe William Trotter, *The Great Migration in Historical Perspective: New Dimensions of Race, Class, and Gender* (Bloomington: Indiana University Press, 1991); Kimberley L. Phillips, *Alabama North: African American Migrants, Community, and Working Class Activism in Cleveland, 1915-1945* (Urbana: University of Illinois Press, 2000).

6 Robert A. Hill and Barbara Bair, *Marcus Garvey: Life and Lessons. A Centennial Companion to the Marcus Garvey and Universal Negro Improvement Association Papers* (Berkeley: University of California Press, 1987), xvii.

7 Michael O. West, "Garveyism in Colonial Zimbabwe, 1924-1936" (unpublished paper in the author's possession), 18.

8 William L. Van Deburg, ed. *Modern Black Nationalism: From Marcus Garvey to Louis Farakhan* (New York: New York University Press, 1997); William Jeremiah Moses, *The Golden Age of Black Nationalism, 1850-1925* (Oxford: Oxford University Press, 1988).

9 Adam Fairclough, *Better Day Coming: Blacks and Equality, 1890-2000* (New York: Viking, 2001), 112.

10 Ibid., 113.

11 For an account of the various contemporary schemes to develop a Black merchant marine, see Ian Duffield, "Pan-Africanism, Rational and Irrational," *Journal of African History* 18 (1977): 602-07; also Rodney Carslile, "Black-Owned Shipping Before Marcus Garvey," *American Neptune* 35:3 (July 1975): 197-206.

12 DNA, RG 65, file OG 388465.

13 Hill, *Garvey Papers*, 1:xlvi-xlvii.

14 Ibid. Robert Hill has noted that Kaba Rega's scheme failed because he lacked access to a propaganda organ like Garvey's *Negro World*.

15 Jeffrey J. Safford, *Wilsonian Maritime Diplomacy 1913-1921* (New Brunswick: Rutgers University Press, 1978). Black shipbuilders were a significant part of this workforce; see George E. Haynes, *The Negro at*

Work During the World War and During Reconstruction (Washington, D.C.: U.S. Department of Labor, Division of Negro Economics, U.S. Government Printing Office, 1921), 58.

16   Samuel A. Lawrence, *United States Merchant Shipping: Policies and Politics* (Washington, D.C.: Brookings Institution, 1966), 40.

17   Lawrence, *U.S. Merchant Shipping*, 41. See also Paul Zeis, *American Shipping Policy* (Princeton: Princeton University Press, 19), 116.

18   Frederick E. Emmons, *American Passenger Ships: The Ocean Lines and Liners, 1873-1983*. (Newark: University of Delaware Press, 1985), 37; Rene De La Pedraja, *The Rise and Decline of American Merchant Shipping in the Twentieth Century* (New York: Twain Press, 1992), 122-23.

19   Hill, *Garvey Papers*, 1:412.

20   *Negro World*, November 6, 1920.

21   Judith Stein, *The World of Marcus Garvey: Race and Class in Modern Society* (Baton Rouge: Louisiana State University Press, 1986), 21.

22   *Negro World*, July 2, 1921.

23   Newspaper report as published in Hill, *Garvey Papers*, 1:411.

24   Fairclough, *Better Day Coming*, 121.

25   The financial records of the Black Star Line were reconstructed by U.S. Government accountants from stock ledgers, cash books, journals, vouchers, and minute books obtained under subpoena on January 5, 1922, as part of Marcus Garvey's mail fraud trial. See DNA, Record Group 267, appellate case no. 30924 "Marcus Garvey vs. USA" government exhibit 134, 2648-2649; government exhibit 138, 2652.

26   "Hodge Kirnon Analyses the Garvey Movement," *Negro World*, January 28, 1923, 7.

27   Fairclough, *Better Day Coming*, 121.

28   For Black participation in World War I, see Arthur E. Barbeau and Florette Henri, *The Unknown Soldiers: Black American Troops in World War I* (Philadelphia: Temple University Press, 1974), especially 78, 176-79; for domestic unrest, see William M. Tuttle Jr., *Race Riot: Chicago in the Red Summer of 1919* (New York: Athenaeum, 1980); for waterfront tensions, see Lester Rubin, *The Negro in the Longshore Industry* (Philadelphia: The Wharton School, University of Pennsylvania; Racial Policies of American Industry, Report No. 2, 1974), 55; for examples of newspaper coverage of Black longshoremen, see "2 Shot in Race Riot by

Longshoremen," *New York Times*, August 17, 1920, and "1,500 in Race Riot at Pier," *New York Times*, September 3, 1920.

29 Frederick S. Harrod, "Jim Crow in the Navy (1798-1941)," *Naval Institute Proceedings* 105 (September 1979): 50-52; excerpts from letters exchanged between Cleveland G. Allen and Secretary of the Navy Josephus Daniels, as quoted in Morris J. McGregor and Bernbard C. Nalty, eds., *Blacks in the United States Armed Forces: Basic Documents* (Wilmington, Delaware: Scholarly Resources, Inc., 1977), 3: 371; Lorenzo J. Greene and Carter G. Woodson, *The Negro Wage Earner* (Washington, D.C.: Association for the Study of Negro Life and History, Inc., 1930), 349; United States Department of Labor, Bureau of Labor Statistics, *Handbook of American Trade Unions* (Washington, D.C.: U.S. Government Printing Office, 1926, Miscellaneous Series No. 240), 94-95; Papers of the United States Shipping Board, Record Group 32, as quoted in Joe W. Trotter and Earl Lewis, eds., *African Americans in the Industrial Age: A Documentary History, 1915-1945* (Evanston, Illinois: Northwestern University Press, 1996), 78-79.

30 Trotter and Lewis, *African Americans in the Industrial Age*, 115-16.

31 Circular illustrated in Milton H. Watson, "Black Star Line," *Steamboat Bill*, 46, 4 (Winter 1989): 269. The article contains numerous inaccuracies; however, the illustrations such as this circular are valuable to the study of the popular appeal of the Black Star Line.

32 Hill, *Garvey Papers*, 2:274; excerpts from the *Emancipator* from April 3 and April 10, 1920, in Hill, *Garvey Papers*, 2:272-279; see also Cockburn's testimony in Marcus Garvey vs. USA (2nd Circ 8317) 292; Hill and Bair, *Marcus Garvey*, 370.

33 Hill, *Garvey Papers*, 2:275.

34 Hugh Mulzac, *A Star to Steer By* (New York: International Publishers, 1963), 76-77.

35 Marcus Garvey vs the US (8317) 58-61; Interview with Paul Morris, author of unpublished study of Crowell and Thurlow, downloaded July 2000 from http://www.yesterdaysisland.com/features/sea_2.html; "Calls Garvey Good Orator, Poor Businessman, and a Robber," *New York Amsterdam News*, May 30, 1923.

36 Known for publicity purposes as the *Frederick Douglass*, the *Yarmouth* was never officially registered under a new name; even in UNIA internal documents she remained *Yarmouth*. W.E.B. Dubois cites this omission in his editorial campaign against Garvey; see "Marcus Garvey" in *Crisis*, 3 (January 1921):113. See also Hill, *Garvey Papers*, 4:428-29.

37 Hill, *Garvey Papers*, 4:183-85, 192; and 2:197-98.

38 See Hill, *Garvey Papers*, 4:427-30, for a detailed chronicle of the *Yarmouth*'s career in the Black Star Line; Malcolm F. Willoughby, *Rum War at Sea* (Washington, D.C.: U.S. Government Printing Office, 1964), 8-20; Hill and Bair, *Marcus Garvey*, 445-46. The loss of the whisky cargo has often been attributed to a drunken crew; however, the *United States Coast Guard Reports of Assistance Rendered* makes no comment as to the condition of the crew; see USCG RAR T720 roll 20, as quoted by Richard W. Peuser, National Archives, in letter to Marifrances Trivelli, July 12, 2000.

39 Mulzac, *Star to Steer By*, 82-87.

40 Hugh Mulzac, "Why the Black Star Line Failed," *Cleveland Journal and Gazette*, October 6, 1923. See also Hill, *Garvey Papers*, 4:431-32, for the background of another ill-fated Black Star Line vessel, the *Shadyside*.

41 Mulzac, *A Star to Steer By*, 92.

42 Hill and Blair, *Marcus Garvey*, 400; Hill, *Garvey Papers*, 4:151-52; Marcus Garvey vs. USA (2nd Circ 8317), 468-69; *Merchant Vessels of the United States*, 1910.

43 Mulzac, *A Star to Steer By*, 92-93. The following year, a bitter Mulzac wrote a series of articles for the *Cleveland Journal & Gazette*; see Hugh Mulzac, "Why the Black Star Line Failed," *Cleveland Journal & Gazette*, September 29-October 27, 1923. He also elaborated on a third Black Star Line vessel, the excursion boat *Shadyside*.

44 Editorial Letter, *Negro World*, July 8, 1922, as published in Hill, *Garvey Papers*, 5:39-40.

45 Editorial Letter, *Negro World*, May 22, 1923, as published in Hill, *Garvey Papers*, 5:312-13. The steamship line idea was resuscitated in the form of the Black Cross Navigation Company, another ill-fated venture; see Hill, *Garvey Papers*, especially 5 and 6.

46 John Gorley Bunker, *Liberty Ships* (Salem: Ayer Company, 1988), 7, 40.; U.S. Maritime Service Veterans, *African-Americans in the U.S. Merchant Marine and U.S. Maritime Service During World War II*, downloaded from http://www.usmm.org/african-americans.html, February 18, 2002.

47 "Spirit of Democracy Shines Bright as *Booker T. Washington* Launched," *Calship Log* (Wilmington, California: Publication of the California Shipbuilding Corporation, October 9, 1942), 9.

48 Mulzac, *A Star to Steer By*, 155-56.

49 Ibid., 153-54.

50 The *Frederick Douglass* was torpedoed by the German submarine U-238 on September 20, 1943. There were no casualties. See Arthur Moore, *A Careless Word, A Needless Sinking* (Kings Point, New York: American Merchant Marine Museum, 1998), 107.

51 See John Beecher, *All Brave Sailors* (New York: Fischer, 1945), for a first-hand account of sailing on the *Booker T. Washington* under Captain Mulzac.

52 After the war, African American officers in the merchant marine were "released from duty" or worked in the engine room, making the victories of Mulzac, Richardson, et al. all the more poignant. See Steven D. Smith and James A. Zeidler, *A Historic Context for the African American Military Experience* (Champaign Illinois: U.S. Army Construction Engineering Laboratories, 1998), 11.

Stilwell

1 Walter H. Beale, "Rhetorical Performative Discourse: A New Theory of Epideictic," *Philosophy and Rhetoric* 11, 4 (1978): 221-46.

2 John M. Bryden, *Tourism and Development: A Case Study Of The Commonwealth Caribbean* (London: Cambridge University Press, 1973).

3 J. Richard. Chase, "The Classical Conception of Epideictic," *The Quarterly Journal of Speech* 47 (1961): 293-300.

4 Celeste Michelle Condit, "The Functions of Epideictic: The Boston Massacre Orations as Exemplar," *Communication Quarterly* 33, 4 (1985): 284-99.

5 Scott Consigny, "Gorgias's Use of the Epideictic," *Philosophy and Rhetoric* 25, 3 (1992): 281- 97.

6 Hector Lennox Crombie, "The Expectations, Desires, and Behaviour of Tourists," in H. J. Prakke and H. M. G. Prakke, eds., *Tourism In The Caribbean: Essays On Problems In Connection With Its Promotion* (Assen, Netherlands: Royal Vangorcum, 1964), 14-44.

7 Catherine A. Lutz, and Jane L. Collins. *Reading National Geographic* (Chicago: University of Chicago, 1993).

8 Carmen L. McCornack, "Publicity's Role in Tourism."

9 Prakke and Prakke, *Tourism in the Caribbean*, 82-96; Carleton Mitchell, "*Carib* Cruises the West Indies," *National Geographic* 93 (1948): 1-50.

10 Carleton Mitchell, email to author. August 14, 2000.

11 Carleton Mitchell, email to author. August 18, 2000.

12 Carleton Mitchell, Oral History Interview 1997, Audiocasette OH 97-9. G. W. Blunt White Library, Mystic Seaport.

13 Oravec, Christine. "'Observation' in Aristotle's Theory of Epideictic," *Philosophy and Rhetoric* 9, 3 (1976): 162-74.

14 Prakke and Prakke, *Tourism In The Caribbean*.

15 Lawrence W. Rosenfield, "The Practical Celebration of Epideictic," in Eugene E. White, ed., *Rhetoric in Transition: Studies in the Nature and Uses of Rhetoric* (University Park: Pennsylvania State University Press, 1980), 131-55.

16 Lois S. Self, "Rhetoric and Phronesis: The Aristotelian Ideal," *Philosophy and Rhetoric* 12,2 (1979): 130-45.

17 Dale Sullivan, "The Ethos of the Epideictic Encounter," *Philosophy and Rhetoric* 26, 2 (1993): 113-33.

18 Omar Swartz, *The View From On The Road: The Rhetorical Vision of Jack Kerouac* (Carbondale: Southern Illinois University Press, 1999).

Nauer

1 John K. Bettersworth, *Mississippi: A History* (Austin, Texas: The Steck Company, 1959), 74; Pearl Vivian Guyton, *The History of Mississippi* (New York: Iroquois Publishing Company, 1935), 43.

2 Charles L. Sullivan, *The Mississippi Gulf Coast: Portrait of a People* (Northridge, California: Windsor Publications, 1985), 59.

3 Ibid., 103-05.

4 David A. Sheffield and Darnell L. Nicovich, *When Biloxi Was the Seafood Capital of the World* (Biloxi: City of Biloxi, 1979), 2 , 35-37.

5 Sullivan, *The Mississippi Gulf Coast*, 116.

6 Ibid., 117; Sheffield and Nicovich, *When Biloxi Was the Seafood Capital*, 5.

7 Sullivan, *The Mississippi Gulf Coast*, 116-19; Aimee Schmidt, "Down Around Biloxi: Culture and Identity in the Biloxi Seafood Industry," in *Mississippi Folklife* 28 (1995), accessed at http://www.edu/depts/south/publish/missfolk/backissues/biloxi.htmil, 4.

8 Sullivan, *The Mississippi Gulf Coast*, 117-20.

9 *Biloxi Daily Herald*, January 11, 1890; Murella Hebert Powell, "Biloxi, Queen City of the Gulf Coast," in *Marine Resources and History of the Mississippi Gulf Coast: History, Art, and Culture of the Mississippi Gulf Coast*, 1 (Jackson, Mississippi: Mississippi Department of Marine Resources, 1998), 142-43; Amelia "Sis" Eleuteris, Oral History Interview, June 1975, Biloxi Public Library Oral History Collection; C. Paige Gutierrez, *The Mississippi Coast and Its People, A History for Students* (Biloxi: Bureau of Marine Resources, Marine Discovery Series, 1987), 9-10. Eleuteris began working in Ernest Desporte's seafood factory at the age of 12 and has lived in Biloxi all of her life. However, other sources, such as Sheffield and Nicovich, *When Biloxi Was the Seafood Capital of the World*, 10, and Schmidt in "Down Around Biloxi," 4, maintain that the seafood factory owners paid the train passage for the itinerant workers.

10 Schmidt, "Down Around Biloxi," 5.

11 Sheffield and Nicovich, *When Biloxi Was the Seafood Capital of the World*, 26, 67; United States Department of the Interior, *Historical Catch Statistics*, compiled by Charles H. Lyle (Washington, D.C.: U.S. Government Printing Office, 1967), 21. In 1896, the Mississippi Legislature granted to the three Boards of Supervisors in Harrison, Jackson, and Hancock Counties (the three Mississippi Coast counties) the full authority to preserve and protect oysters, crabs, saltwater fish, and shrimp. In 1902, the Board of Oyster Commissioners supervised all aspects of oyster harvesting after its creation in 1902 by the Mississippi State Legislature. By 1930, the Mississippi Seafood Commission was empowered by the Mississippi State Legislature to have jurisdiction over all aspects of seafood, living or existing, in Mississippi maritime waters. The Oyster Commission then transferred all powers to the Mississippi Seafood Commission. An outline of laws governing Mississippi's marine resources can be further studied in Michael W. Janus, "Selected Laws Affecting Mississippi and the Gulf of Mexico Marine Resources," in *Marine Resources and History of the Mississippi Gulf Coast*, 3 (Jackson: Mississippi Department of Marine Resources, 1998).

12 Department of Commerce, *List of Merchant Vessels of the United States, 1914* (Washington, D.C.: U.S. Government Printing Office, 1914); Russell E. Barnes, "The Impact on Work and Culture in Biloxi Boatbuilding 1890-1930 (Master's thesis, University of Southern Mississippi, 1997), 95; JoLyn Covacevich and Jack Covacevich, telephone interview by author, January 20, 2003. The Covacevich family has been involved in Biloxi boatbuilding for generations and, therefore, closely involved with the changing boat styles and demands of the local seafood industry. The Covacevich Yacht & Sail Company still operates in Biloxi.

13 Schmidt, "Down Around Biloxi," 5; Sullivan, *The Mississippi Gulf Coast*, 118; Ray Thompson, "The Story of the Slavonians," *Know Your Coast*, 1957. Ethnic Groups Vertical File, Biloxi Public Library.

14 Sheffield and Nicovich, *When Biloxi Was the Seafood Capital*, 29-35; Julius Lopez interview, *Biloxi Press*, September 5, 1979.

15 Sullivan, *The Mississippi Gulf Coast*, 145; Powell, "Biloxi, Queen City of the Gulf Coast," 146.

16 Schmidt, "Down Around Biloxi," 6.

17 Ellison Hebert, interview by author, June 13, 1996, Ocean Springs, Mississippi.

18 Kat Bergeron, "The Point Offers Vivid Americana," *Biloxi Sun Herald*, February 11, 2001.

19 Thompson, "The Story of the Slavonians."

20 Ibid. The new Lodge was built in 1938 and cost $25,000. Steve Kuljis was president, Vincent Kuluz was vice president, and Tony M. Pitalo was the secretary-treasurer.

21 Ray Thompson, "Why the Fleur de Lis Society of Biloxi was Founded," in *Know Your Coast*, 1957. Ethnic Groups Vertical File, Biloxi Public Library. The original members of the Fleur-de-Lis Society were August Bairilaux, August Theroit, Adam Boudreaux, Jake Broussard, Xavier Boudwin, Alcee Broussard, Oliver Romero, Ben Hebert, Laurent Smith, Lesson Broussard, Clomer Leaux, Seagus Leaux, Fernando Smith, Adolph Romero, Noah Broussard, Laurent Duplain, Wallace Vallo, P.A. Songe, Homer Barras, James Higgenbotham, Arthur Broussard, Horace Mouton, Lucian Olier, and Lucian Arcenaux.

22 Stephanie C. Richmond and David Alfred Wheeler, *The Growth of the Biloxi Public School System* 1 (Biloxi: City of Biloxi, 1979), 6.

23 Ibid., 58.

24 Sullivan, *The Mississippi Gulf Coast*, 147; Powell, "Biloxi, Queen City of the Gulf Coast," 152-54; Deanne Stephens Nuwer and Michael Sicuro, *The Buildings of Biloxi: An Architectural Survey*, 2nd ed. (Biloxi: City of Biloxi, 2000), 21.

25 Nuwer and Sicuro, *The Buildings of Biloxi*, 22; Sullivan, *The Mississippi Gulf Coast*, 158.

26 Harvey Arden, "The Wanderers from Vung Tau, Troubled Odyssey of Vietnamese Fishermen," *National Geographic* 160 (September 1981): 380-81.

27 Ibid., 378.

28 Ibid., 384.

29 Keith Burton, "Stricter rules, competition are biggest factors in shifting business," *Biloxi Sun Herald*, April 30, 1999; Patrick Peterson, "Traditions Endure," *Biloxi Sun Herald*, April 30, 1999. Both of these clippings are in the Seafood Industry Vertical File, Biloxi Public Library, Biloxi, Mississippi.

30 Schmidt, "Down Around Biloxi," 9-10.

31 Schmidt, "Down Around Biloxi," 8; Nuwer and Sicuro, *Architectural History of Biloxi*, 94, 102.

32 One need only to travel down Howard Avenue in Biloxi to experience the cultural triangle of Biloxi called The Point.

Weintraub

1 Lerone Bennet, *Before the Mayflower: A History of Black America* (New York: Penguin Books, 1987); Joel Spring, *Deculturalization and the Struggle for Equality* (New York: McGraw-Hill, 1997); Ronald Takaki, *A Different Mirror* (New York: Little, Brown, 1993); Howard Zinn, *A People's History of the United States* (New York: Harper & Row, 1995).

2 Adrienne Rich, *Blood, Bread and Poetry, Selected Prose, 1979-85* (New York: W.W. Norton, 1986), 199.

3 Takaki, *A Different Mirror.*

4 Zinn, *A People's History,* 618.

5 Stephen Kemmis and Robin McTaggart, eds., *The Action Research Planner,* 3rd ed. (Geelong, Victoria: Deakin University Press, 1988), 5.

6 Stephen Brookfield, *Becoming a Critically Reflective Teacher* (San Francisco: Jossey-Bass, 1995), 8.

7 Stanley Aronowitz and Henry Giroux, *Postmodern Education: Politics, Culture and Social Criticism* (Minneapolis: University of Minnesota Press, 1991), 100.

8 George H. Moore, *Notes on the History of Slavery in Massachusetts* (New York: Appleton, 1866), 83-87.

9 Elaine Weintraub, "African American History of Martha's Vineyard," *New England Journal of History* 50, 2 (1993): 34-47.

10 Quoted in Elaine Weintraub, *African American Heritage Trail of Martha's Vineyard* (Tisbury, Massachusetts: African American Heritage Trail of Martha's Vineyard, 1997).

11 A. Railton, ed., *Diaries of Jeremiah Pease* (Edgartown: Vineyard Museum, 1983), 27.

12 Remember Cooper, Deposition, August 28, 1851, Barnstable County Court 6563.

13 Railton, *Diaries of Jeremiah Pease*, 45.

14 E.T. Stringer, *Action Research: A Handbook for Practitioners*, 2nd ed. (London: Sage, 1999).

Wolff

1 William A. Owens, *Black Mutiny: The Revolt on the Schooner Amistad* (reprint, New York: Plume, 1997); Barbara Chase-Riboud, *Echo of Lions* (New York: Morrow, 1989); Alexis Pate, *Amistad* (New York: Signet, 1997); David Pesci, *Amistad: A Novel* (New York: Marlowe & Company, 1997); Karen Zeinert, *The Amistad Revolt and American Abolition* (North Haven, Connecticut.: Linnet Books, 1997). Pate's novel was based upon David Franzoni's screenplay for Spielberg's film.

2 *U.S. v. Libelants and Claimants of the Schooner Amistad*, 40 U.S. 518, 518-22; Howard Jones, *Mutiny on the Amistad* (New York: Oxford University Press, 1987), 14-16, 22-29.

3 Bertram Wyatt-Brown, *Lewis Tappan and the Evangelical War Against Slavery* (reprint, Baton Rouge: Louisiana State University Press, 1997), 206, 209; Jones, *Mutiny on the Amistad*, 31-35.

4 Jones, *Mutiny on the Amistad*, 56-60.

5 Ibid., 63-67.

6 Ibid., 76-77.

7 Ibid., 84-93.

8 John Warner Barber, *A History of the Amistad Captives* (New Haven: E.L. & J.W. Barber, 1840), 20.

9   Jones, *Mutiny on the Amistad*, 120-35, 142.

10 Ibid., 171.

11 Ibid., 172-82.

12 Ibid., 188-92.

13 Ibid., 202-05.

14 Wyatt-Brown, *Lewis Tappan*, 205-25; Benjamin Quarles, *Black Abolitionists* (New York: Oxford University Press, 1969), 76-79; Robert Brent Toplin, *History by Hollywood: The Use and Abuse of the American Past* (Urbana and Chicago: University of Illinois Press, 1996), vii-22, quote from vii. Allen had purchased the film rights to Owens's novel in 1984, and later chose Spielberg to co-produce and direct the film. See Joseph McBride, "Free at Last: With Spielberg's *Amistad,* Debbie Allen's Ship Finally Comes In," *Boxoffice Online,* December 1997, http://www.boxoff.com/dec97story3.html (30 June 2002).

15 Eric Foner, "Ken Burns and the Romance of Reunion," and Leon Litwack, "Telling the Story: The Historian, the Filmmaker, and the Civil War," both in *Ken Burns' The Civil War: Historians Respond,* Robert Brent Toplin, ed., (New York: Oxford University Press, 1996), 101-40.

16 Howard Jones, "*Amistad:* Movie, History, and the Academy Awards," *The History Teacher* 31, 3 (May 1998): 380.

17 Folayan Osagie, *The Amistad Revolt: Memory, Slavery, and the Politics of Identity in the United States and Sierra Leone* (Athens: University of Georgia Press, 2000), 127.

18 Sean Wilentz, "The Mandarin and the Rebel: John Quincy Adams, *La Amistad,* and Democracy in America," *The New Republic,* December 22, 1997, 32; Osagie, *Amistad Revolt,* 128.

19 *The African Captives. The Trial of the Prisoners of the Amistad on the Writ of Habeas Corpus, before the Circuit Court of the United States, for the District of Connecticut, at Hartford; Judges Thompson and Judson. September Term, 1839* (New York: n.p., 1839), 42-43.

20 Quoted in Stanley Harrold, *American Abolitionists*, Seminar Studies in History (Essex, England: Longman, 2001), 114-15.

21 Investors in the *Zong* filed an insurance claim to recover the cost of 133 Africans that had been thrown overboard to save on food. The British abolitionist Granville Sharp tried unsuccessfully to have those responsible charged with murder. See David Brion Davis, *The Problem of Slavery in the Age of Revolution, 1770-1823* (Ithaca: Cornell University Press,

1975), 405-06; Seymour Drescher and Stanley L. Engerman, eds., *A Historical Guide to World Slavery* (New York: Oxford University Press, 1998), 69-71.

22 Wyatt-Brown, *Lewis Tappan*, 217-18; James Oliver Horton and Lois E. Horton, *In Hope of Liberty: Culture, Community and Protest Among Northern Free Blacks, 1700-1860* (New York: Oxford University Press, 1997), 244-45.

23 *The Charleston Mercury*, August 28, 1839, reprinting information originally published on August 23, by the *New York Commercial Advertiser*. Microfilm copy in the College of Charleston Library.

24 *Charleston Mercury*, January 22-23, 1840.

25 Barber, *A History of the Amistad Captives*, 24.

26 Ibid., 8-14, 20. "Mr. Fletcher" may be a misnomer for L.N. Fowler, a phrenologist who published a description of Cinque in *American Phrenological Journal and Miscellany* in 1840. See Jones, *Mutiny on the Amistad*, 42-43, 230 fn50.

27 Barber, *A History of the Amistad Captives*, 9, 25.

28 Ibid., 10-11, 25-26.

29 Jones, *Mutiny on the Amistad*, 125. This story strongly resembles that of Grabeau, who was seized for his uncle's debt. See Barber, *A History of the Amistad Captives*, 9.

30 Owens, *Black Mutiny*, 308; Howard Jones, "Cinqué of the *Amistad* a Slave Trader? Perpetuating a Myth," *Journal of American History* 87, 3 (December 2000): 932-39. Jones's article forms the foundation of a roundtable entitled, "Cinqué and the Historians: How a Story Takes Hold," with responses from Finkelman, Wyatt-Brown, and also William McFeely.

31 Barber, *A History of the Amistad Captives*, 9-15; Patrick Manning, *Slavery and African Life: Occidental, Oriental, and African Slave Trades*, African Studies Series No. 67 (Cambridge: Cambridge University Press, 1990), 88-90.

32 Owens, *Black Mutiny*, 62; Chase-Riboud, *Echo of Lions*, 77; Pesci, *Amistad*, 55; Zeinert, *Amistad Slave Revolt*, 16-17; Pate, *Amistad*, 21-22.

33 Barber, *A History of the Amistad Captives*, 19; Wyatt-Brown, *Lewis Tappan*, 158-60; Horton and Horton, *In Hope of Liberty*, 240.

34 Henry Louis Gates Jr., *Classic Slave Narratives* (New York: Mentor, 1987), 33, 37. As this volume uses an 1814 edition of *The Interesting Life of Olaudah Equiano*, I have also consulted an online copy of the 1789 edition available through *Documenting the American South*, University of North Carolina at Chapel Hill Libraries, 7 December 2001, http://docsouth.unc.edu/neh/equiano1/equiano1.html#p45, 72, 85 (June 30, 2002).

35 Franklin W. Knight, *Slave Society in Cuba During the Nineteenth Century* (Madison: University of Wisconsin Press, 1970), chaps. 1-3, especially 47-54.

36 C. Peter Ripley, ed., *The Black Abolitionist Papers. Volume III: The United States, 1830-1846* (Chapel Hill: University of North Carolina Press, 1991), 189-94; Chris Dixon, *Perfecting the Family: Antislavery Marriages in Nineteenth-Century America* (Amherst: University of Massachusetts Press, 1997), 97-101.

37 W. Jeffrey Bolster, *Black Jacks: African American Seamen in the Age of Sail* (Cambridge, Massachusetts.: Harvard University Press, 1997); Peter P. Hinks, *To Awaken My Afflicted Brethren: David Walker and the Problem of Antebellum Slave Resistance* (University Park: Pennsylvania State University Press, 1997), 160-69.

38 Horton and Horton, *In Hope of Liberty*, 203-36; Kathryn Grover, *The Fugitive's Gibraltar: Escaping Slaves and Abolitionism in New Bedford, Massachusetts* (Amherst: University of Massachusetts Press, 2001); Barber, *A History of the Amistad Captives*, 6; *The African Captives. The Trial of the Prisoners of the Amistad*, 29.

39 40 U.S. 518, at 593; Joseph Story, *Commentaries on the Constitution of the United States*, 4th ed., with notes and additions by Thomas M. Cooley, 2 vols. (Boston: Little, Brown, 1873), 2: 449-57 [1663-73].

40 40 U.S. 518, at 592-93.

41 Ibid., at 593-95. Gilpin's reference to "the intercourse of nations" is at 541.

42 Jones, *Mutiny on the Amistad*, 12-13; Charles Francis Adams, ed., *Memoirs of John Quincy Adams, Comprising Portions of His Diary from 1795 to 1848*, 10 vols. (Philadelphia: J.B. Lippincott & Co., 1874-77), 10:373.

43 Inga Clendinnen, *Ambivalent Conquests: Maya and Spaniard in Yucatan, 1517-1570* (Cambridge: Cambridge University Press, 1987), ix.

Index